Using Libraries

An informative guide for students and general users

By the same author

Dictionaries (1966)

Using Libraries

An informative guide for students
and general users

Kenneth Whittaker

Fellow of the Library Association

 ANDRE DEUTSCH/A Grafton Book

First published 1961 by
André Deutsch Limited
105 Great Russell Street London wc1

Copyright © 1961, 1963, 1972 by Kenneth Whittaker
Second (revised) edition 1963
Third (revised) edition 1972

Printed in Great Britain by
Ebenezer Baylis and Son Limited
The Trinity Press Worcester and London

isbn 0 233 96358 8

Contents

6   *Contents*

Illustrations

For permission to reproduce the plates in this book the author and publishers acknowledge their thanks to: the County Librarian, Wiltshire County Council Library and Museum Service (photo: West) for plate 1; Wandsworth Public Libraries for plate 2; Lincoln Public Library for plates 3 and 8; North Riding County Library for plate 4; Leicester City Libraries for plate 5; Liverpool City Libraries for plate 7; London Borough of Camden for plates 6 and 9; London Borough of Hackney for plate 10; the Library Association for plate 11 and the British Institute of Management for plate 12.

Preface to third edition

I have not only up-dated the contents, but made some revisions and additions to the text. Chapter 1 has been considerably altered in content, whilst whole sections have been added to chapters 4 and 5. The number of illustrations has been increased, and all the photographs in the earlier editions replaced by new ones. The Appendix on the Dewey Classification scheme has been retained but rearranged.

I should like to thank both my father and Mr K. Lund, FLA, for reading the manuscript and for making suggestions that have improved it. I am also indebted to my father for executing the drawings which appear within the text.

The preparation of this third edition has been helped by several of my fellow lecturers at the Manchester School of Librarianship reading through various parts of material I have added. I should like to thank them for their comments.

KENNETH WHITTAKER, *August 1971*

Introduction

The purpose of this book is to present the resources and services that libraries have to offer, and indicate how best to use them. It is aimed at all people who either need or want to use libraries intelligently. It will appeal, I hope, to members of the general public, to older schoolchildren, to students and to teachers. It should also appeal to entrants to the library profession, giving them some idea of the world they are entering. Previous knowledge of the working of libraries is not needed in order to understand the contents of this book.

It is surprising how little has been written on the subject of using libraries. A number of libraries have produced guides for the use of their readers, but virtually nothing has recently been published on using libraries as a whole. Yet there is obviously room for general guides like this book, as well as for guides to individual libraries. Libraries have an important place in our civilization, and it is vital that their place should be appreciated and their resources and services used to the full. Many people still think that libraries are collections of dog-eared and out-of-date books, fit only to be read by those with nothing better to do. It will be quite obvious to anybody who digs into the pages of this work that such an idea is completely behind the times.

Libraries are primarily important because they are reservoirs of knowledge. They are places where research is carried out, the research workers tapping and considering the knowledge made available. The word research usually conjures up in the mind a picture of a laboratory, with workers in white coats carefully carrying test-tubes; but, taking all fields of knowledge into consideration, more research is done in libraries than in laboratories. Libraries are also powerful contributors to the spread of education. They supplement the work of the teacher and they educate those who have no teacher. The importance of the library in the work of schools and colleges is gradually becoming appreciated. One result of this is the growing demand that the library should be the central feature of new school and college buildings. The work of the library in enabling people to educate themselves has long been appreciated. In the United States earlier this century millions of immigrants from all the countries of Europe had to be integrated into the American way of life and taught the English language. The public library is considered to have played a decisive part in educating them. Libraries are also places where information can quickly be found on virtually every subject. The problems confronting the chemist in his experiments, and the problems confronting the boy making his own model aeroplane have one thing in common; they can be solved by visiting a library.

The contents of libraries not only supply knowledge, they also provide pleasure. Reading is one of the most popular of hobbies and libraries can supply books to suit all tastes. The supply of books to provide pleasure is one of the principal functions of many types of library, particularly those catering for people, like hospital patients, living in situations where some of the pleasures of life are denied them.

The importance of libraries has been stressed because it needs stressing. Libraries contain books, together with matter supplementing books, such as periodicals. For their contents, collectively called library materials, there is no substitute.

I should like to make one final point before concluding this introduction. The information contained in the following pages is based on library organization and practice in Great Britain. However, much of what is written applies to libraries in other countries of the English-speaking world. As there has always been close contact between British librarians and those in the United States and the Commonwealth, libraries in these countries have much in common.

Chapter 1
Libraries and library use

The library world

There are two kinds of library, one dead, the other alive. This book is concerned only with the second kind. Perhaps no library is really dead, for where there are books both knowledge and pleasure are always to be found. The term may reasonably be applied, however, to those libraries that are no longer expanding, having been founded in times far different from our own, and having been unable to keep up with the changing world.

There are only a few libraries in this category, most of them belonging to either the Cathedral and Parish library group or the Circulating and Subscription library group. The former group once served an important purpose, to keep the clergy informed. Now, they are primarily of historical interest. The latter group, a type of library normally run on a commercial basis and catering, on the whole, for those people who want to borrow the latest popular books, has in the last few years become almost extinct because of the success of public libraries and the growth of paperback publishing. The most famous library of this group that remains is the London Library. This, however, is not a typical Circulating or Subscription library as it is scholarly in character. Thomas Carlyle was one of its founders, and leading literary figures have been members ever since.

The libraries that are alive can be divided into six groups. Each of these groups will now be briefly examined.

I. NATIONAL LIBRARIES

National libraries are so called because they are financed by the government of a country and exist to serve the nation as a whole. They are usually very large libraries, probably stocking millions of books. Their main purpose is to collect and preserve the books and other printed matter produced in the country. To aid them in their task, they are usually given the privilege of legal deposit. This means that it is laid down by the law of the country that a copy of every book published in it must be sent free of charge to them. In Great Britain there are three main national libraries, the British Museum in London, the National Library of Scotland in Edinburgh, and the National Library of Wales in Aberystwyth. The British Museum is deservedly one of the most famous libraries of the world, but it is comparatively small and undeveloped compared with the national library of the United States, the Library of Congress in Washington, or with the Lenin State Library in Moscow.

In addition to the three British national libraries named above, there is in this country the National Reference Library of Science and Invention in London, and the National Lending Library for Science and Technology at Boston Spa in Yorkshire. Both these libraries are recent foundations. The former, based on the Patent Office Library, is part of the British Museum. The latter is a most unusual national library, as its main purpose is not to preserve its stock, but to lend it by post to libraries. Incidentally, its scope is now wider than science and technology, as it also stocks periodical publications on the social sciences.

Ambitious plans for reorganizing Britain's national libraries were put to the government in 1971. In a few years' time there will be a British Library of which both the British Museum and the National Lending Library will form a part. The reference services of this British Library will be located in London, the lending services at Boston Spa.

2. UNIVERSITY LIBRARIES

University libraries are of three kinds: old foundations that have, because of their age, built up resources comparable with those of many national libraries; later, mainly nineteenth-century, foundations, that have rather smaller stocks; and post-World War II foundations that have, as yet, barely sufficient resources to carry out their various functions.

In England, the most famous libraries of the first kind are the university libraries of Oxford and Cambridge. The present library at Oxford, the Bodleian, was founded by Sir Thomas Bodley as long ago as 1602; the Cambridge University Library dates, though not in its present form, from even earlier. These two libraries, because of their status, have the right by law to demand a copy of any book published in Great Britain.

There are many university libraries of the second kind, because the first big expansion in university education was in the nineteenth century. The university libraries of Manchester, Liverpool and Nottingham are typical examples.

University foundations of the third kind include a number of institutions, such as Loughborough, that were previously Colleges of Advanced Technology, though most, like the University of Lancaster, have been universities from their foundation. The book stocks of these new university libraries may be small but they are leading most of the older ones in the services they offer their readers.

3. COLLEGE LIBRARIES

It is not difficult to detect the difference between a university and a college library. Both cover a wide range of subjects, but the college library carries the smaller stock, and covers its subjects to a less advanced standard. Developing at the moment are the libraries of a new kind of educational institution, the Polytechnic. In the main these will serve students reading for degrees, and will be a cross between college and university libraries.

College libraries, especially those in technical colleges, have increased over the last few years both in number and in size. It may be noted that a number of college libraries, for example those in theological colleges, cover only a specialized field of knowledge, and might be better classed with special libraries.

An interesting feature affecting college libraries in the United States has been the setting up of a number of institutions known as library-colleges. These are colleges that base their teaching on the use of the college library rather than on lectures.

4. SCHOOL LIBRARIES

School libraries vary considerably, as there are many types of school catering for a variety of age-groups. They are, naturally, most developed in comprehensive and grammar schools. Although school libraries are much smaller than most college libraries, they try to have at least a few books on every subject of interest to their pupils. The main purpose of school libraries, as of college libraries, is to further education, but school libraries usually cater as well for recreational needs. To supplement their resources, in many areas they borrow collections of books from local public libraries.

School libraries sometimes stock not only books and periodicals but also the audio-visual materials held by the school. This has led, in recent years, to the setting up of what are usually known as multi-media resource centres. No doubt more school libraries will enlarge their functions and change their name as the use of tape recordings (including video-tapes) and programmed learning kits expands.

5. PUBLIC LIBRARIES

Public libraries are controlled by local councils, financed out of the rates, and available for everybody to use. They came into being when Parliament passed the Public Libraries Act of 1850. Curiously enough, although this Act allowed public money to be spent on staff and buildings, it did not permit money to be spent on buying books. It was thought that these would be given by local citizens. Public libraries expanded slowly at first, but today they offer a wide range of services and have service points in every town and county. Public libraries are commonly divided into municipal and county libraries, but the difference between the two is virtually limited to the way they are controlled. Municipal libraries are controlled by the local council, county libraries by the county council. There is some variation in the standard of service provided by public libraries as some councils are able and prepared to spend more money on them than others. However, the 1964 Public Libraries Act has led to an improvement in the poorer libraries, has encouraged the general raising of standards, and has increased the central government's library powers. From 1974 there will be fewer (but bigger) public libraries as a result of the reorganization of local government boundaries.

6. SPECIAL LIBRARIES

This group is a large and varied one. It may, indeed, be split into three, as the term special libraries covers those libraries dealing with special subjects, those catering for special types of reader, and those whose interest is in special library materials rather than in books.

There are a large number of libraries dealing with special subjects: the libraries of industrial firms, the libraries of government departments, the libraries of research associations, the libraries of societies and professional bodies. The library of the Metal Box Company, of the Department of Trade and Industry, of the British Iron and Steel Research Association, of the Royal Geographical Society, are representative examples. The larger public libraries often have technical departments and other collections of specialized material, and these are sometimes termed special libraries; they are more correctly called subject or special departments.

There is a large number of libraries that cater for special types of reader, such as hospital patients, those on board ship, and the blind. The British Red Cross Society, the Seafarers' Welfare Society and the National Library for the Blind, do much to cater for the three types of reader mentioned.

The third category of special library is less common, but there are libraries that deal in the main with illustrations, cuttings, gramophone records, films, and the like, rather than with books. The libraries belonging to newspaper companies contain books, but they are more concerned with newspaper cuttings and with illustrations; the Library of the British Institute of Recorded Sound deals principally with gramophone records, and that of the British Film Institute with films.

Related to special libraries, and therefore commented on here, are information bureaux. Indeed, the professional association that caters for special libraries, Aslib, was previously called the Association of Special Libraries and Information Bureaux. If a distinction can be drawn between a special library and an information bureau, it is that the latter will have too small a stock really to be considered a library, and that its function is to put enquirers into contact with people and organizations that can help them, rather than to answer their enquiries from its own resources. Whilst the majority of information bureaux, like that of the British Lighting Council, are connected in some way with industry, some towns run them as part of their town hall service.

Although the library world is many sided, the various types of libraries described have much in common. In addition, most types of libraries lend books to other types, and staff are constantly moving from one kind of library to another.

There are several organized systems for the interlending of books and other library materials. The scheme based on the National Central Library in London and that organized by the National Lending Library for Science and Technology are the two most important. Further information is given on these schemes in the next chapter. In addition to organized interlending of books, there are other forms of co-operation between libraries, some of them quite informal. For example, if a library has a difficult enquiry that it finds it cannot answer from its own stock, then another bigger or more specialized library will be approached, and will supply the answer.

Staff can easily move to jobs in other kinds of libraries because the qualifications established for librarians by the Library Association are generally accepted. The Library Association is the most important professional organization in the field of librarianship, though there are a number of more specialized organizations, such as the School Library Association. Libraries and librarians are also linked together internationally. There is an International Association of Library Associations, there is the work of UNESCO for libraries, and there are also the more informal links forged through the considerable number of librarians who visit or even obtain posts in other countries.

Factors affecting the use of libraries

Why do some people use libraries more than others, and why are some libraries easier to use than other libraries? These questions, together with related ones, are now considered. The answers are fairly obvious when thought about, but it is only when they are systematically set down that they can be seen clearly. The factors affecting the use of libraries determine whether a library is used at all, and whether it is used regularly, as well as whether it can be used efficiently. Most attention will be paid, however, to efficient use.

I. USE V. NON-USE

Many people have libraries available to them that they do not use. Public libraries, for example, are available to all members of a community, but only about 25 per cent will be registered borrowers at any one time. Admittedly, public libraries can be used for some purposes by people not registered as members, but the figure of 25 per cent is so low that obviously many people do not use their public libraries (or indeed any library) at all. What are the reasons?

The following may not be the only reasons, but they are five important ones. First, people do not use libraries because they are not interested in books and reading. Perhaps they are not interested because their reading ability is poor; they find books difficult to follow and can get no enjoyment from them. Perhaps they are not interested because they believe that reading is a waste of time. Such people are, of course, the kind who, if they see one of their children reading, shout 'Stop reading that book and do something useful.'

A second reason for non-use is lack of time. Now it is true that if we want to do something badly enough, we find time to do it. However, lack of time is a genuine reason for many people not using libraries at some periods in their lives. They will use libraries as children and as students, but when they start courting, marrying, and raising a family, there is no longer time (except for the really keen reader) to visit the library. Surveys of public library use have revealed that the number of people in a community who have been members is as great as the number who are currently members. In a few years, some of the ex-members will have rejoined the library and some of the present members left, all because of changes in personal commitments.

A third reason is that reading matter is obtained from sources other than libraries. If a sample of book readers were asked where they had obtained the book they are reading, only about half would reply that they had borrowed it from a library. The rest would reply that they had borrowed it from a friend or relation or that they had bought the book. With the number of paperbacks available today, it is possible for some book readers to afford to buy all they read. However, most book buyers are also book borrowers, and probably library members as well.

The fourth reason why libraries are not used is because people do not know what they offer. True, most people know that books can be borrowed, but they know nothing of the other services public libraries have available. They don't know, for example, that they can obtain information, such as the addresses of societies and organizations, from their local library. The Brian Groombridge report *The Londoner and his library* revealed that as many as 55 per cent of the people who had never been members did not know that public libraries offered information services. The person who is not a keen reader and therefore not a library member may fail to use his library when he could, it seems, merely because he does not know what services it offers him.

A comment on knowledge of non-public libraries is called for at this point. It is not generally known that many non-public libraries may be used by the public. Admittedly, there may be conditions laid down, and the services offered will normally be limited, but for reference or research purposes their doors are open.

The final reason for non-use is of a different type from those so far considered. It stems not from the library user but from the libraries being inconveniently sited, or open only at unsuitable times.

II. REGULAR V. IRREGULAR USE

The reasons why people use libraries rarely when they could be using them frequently overlap with the reasons for non-use.

One reason for irregular use (rather than non-use) is dissatisfaction with the library. Most library users are long-suffering (perhaps too much so). However, a few become dissatisfied with the rules, or with there being too few new books. As for those keen readers who use more than a single library in order to obtain all they require, they obviously use less the libraries that they find have least to offer.

Of course, reasons for irregular use can stem from reading habits and have nothing to do with the library. A number of readers are infrequent library users because they only visit a library when they have a particular need or problem. Perhaps they want to look something up in connection with their job, or they want to borrow a book to help them with their latest hobby. Then, and only then, do they come into the library. Other readers are irregular in the use they make of libraries because they visit the library just at certain times of the year. University students enter it only when at home during the vacations. Seaside landladies use it only in the winter when they have time to relax.

III. EFFICIENT V. INEFFICIENT USE

Efficient use of a library, because it is important enough to be discussed at length, will be divided into four headed sections. Each deals with a major factor.

1. *Reader's knowledge*

A reader's knowledge of a library is based on several things. It is based on his experience of that library. It is based on his experience of other libraries. It is affected by whether he has been given any information about the library, e.g. a pamphlet guide to it. It is affected by whether he has undergone formal training in the use of libraries.

Obviously experience makes for efficiency. If a library has been used for some time, then a fair amount of information about it will have been gleaned. Experience of other libraries may also help, as what has been learnt about one library can often be applied to another.

The information a reader may be given to help him make full use of a library can take several forms. It can take the form of publications, such as the pamphlet guide already mentioned. It can take the form of staff assistance. It can take the form of visual aids, such as a plan of the library displayed in the library entrance. In the future, there may increasingly be tape-recorded guidance.

Formal training in the use of books and libraries is being carried out now in a large number of libraries, especially those of universities and colleges. Indeed there is a type of librarian known as a tutor-librarian who specializes in this work. Training of readers, one of the services that libraries offer, is described in the next chapter.

2. *Type of library*

Some types of library are more difficult to use than others and, on the whole, special libraries are the most difficult. There are two reasons for this. First, special libraries are usually quite different from each other, so that knowledge of one does not help much when it comes to using another. (With most other types of library, individual libraries have much in common with other libraries of the same type, and so knowledge of one does help considerably when it comes to using another.)

The second reason why special libraries tend to be the hardest to use is that their stock consists principally of non-book materials, periodicals, pamphlets, patents, etc. The whole layout and arrangement is therefore different from that of book-dominated libraries. The shelving is specialized, the classification and cataloguing unusual, the total appearance strange. In fact, with knowledge and experience, special libraries can be used extremely efficiently, especially as they are generally fairly small, and their staffs offer good reader assistance.

3. *Size of library*

Readers using national libraries, the largest libraries of all, university libraries and the central buildings of city public libraries, find that such large libraries present them with special problems.

The first is that of size itself. It takes a long time to reach what you want in a large building, and it takes a long time to locate a particular title because the stock is that much bigger. Finding a required title often poses readers with a second and more troublesome problem. Many big libraries have the majority of their stock on closed-access. This means that it is kept on shelves open only to members of the staff. To obtain a book from such shelves, it is usually necessary to fill in a form giving details of the desired book (including its shelf number as given in the library's catalogue), and to hand the form to a member of the library staff. The book may then be brought to a seat that the reader has chosen, or the reader may have to go to the library counter to collect it. The main value, from the library's point of view, of keeping material on closed-access is that it saves space. Space is a tremendous problem for libraries with large stocks, as they are constantly adding considerable quantities of new material to what they already have, and the pace of their accessions has been increasing for some years now as the world's output of books and periodicals increases. Harvard University library, indeed, stated some time ago that it expected its stock to double every ten years.

Another problem to do with obtaining a required title in a large library is that the stock on a particular subject may not all be in the same department or even in the same building. Of course, even in fairly small libraries, such as public library branches, there is sometimes a separate reference department and the work you want may be shelved there and not in the lending library. However, in large libraries there are further places where titles may be shelved. They may be kept in reserve, on closed-access as we have called it. They may be in a special collection (large libraries are rich in these), stored in its own room. They may be in an overflow library building such as the British Museum's Reading Room and Store at Colindale.

In recent years, the central libraries of larger towns have developed along subject department lines. This means that instead of dividing their stock between two departments, one lending, the other reference, they have divided up their stock on a subject basis. The result is several departmental libraries of varying size, each covering a subject such as 'Science and Technology' or 'Music'. For readers, this arrangement has a number of advantages, including the placing together of lending and reference material. However, it also makes for a problem. If you want to borrow or refer to books on several subjects, you will have to tour a number of departments, and getting from one to another in a building of some size can be quite time consuming.

The final problem to be considered under the heading of size is that in most large libraries, except those of the universities, there is comparatively little material that can be borrowed. A high proportion of the library stock is for reference only, a major purpose of large libraries is to aid research by being storehouses of knowledge. If books were lent out, they might be lost from the store and they would certainly wear out more quickly. In addition, research workers who often travel many miles to see material which they know a library possesses would find that journey wasted if the material had been lent out.

So the use of large research libraries poses a number of problems. Most of these are, however, the price that has to be paid for making accessible in one place a wide range of literature.

4. *Standard of service*

A library that offers as many services as possible to its readers, will not only satisfy those readers, it will also be easier to use. For example, if the library is prepared to compile bibliographies and reading lists for its readers, then the user can find out quickly and efficiently exactly what the library has that he wants. Libraries should therefore offer a wide range of services to readers, for by doing so they are not only showing themselves to be good libraries but are aiding their readers to use the library efficiently. However, a good library will not only offer a wide variety of services. Each of the services it offers will be of a high quality. Quality of service is important but it will be found to vary considerably, staff assistance most of all perhaps. Undoubtedly the quality of service offered to readers has improved in recent years, as more libraries have become reader conscious and have tried to provide for them as individuals. Special libraries, especially those of industrial firms, have led the way. They have been able to set the pace as they usually have a high ratio of staff to number of users, and the users demand a high standard of service. In these libraries the staff often have a knowledge of the user's special field as well as of librarianship. This means that they can help him in ways not possible otherwise. They can, for example, make summaries of articles of interest to him. You can only understand articles on, for instance, polymer chemistry or structural engineering if you really know those subjects. Librarians who do, and are therefore subject specialists in addition to being librarians, are sometimes known as Information Officers.

Though the standard of service in libraries generally is

improving, it is not improving in every library. The difficulties that face libraries trying to improve their service in any way are today considerable. One difficulty arises from the continual increase in the production of publications of all kinds. This literature explosion, as it is called, is the result of the ever-increasing amount of knowledge being discovered and reported, especially in science and technology. Now, this increase means that librarians can hardly keep up with selecting and organizing their ever-mounting stock, and they are left little time to work out new ways of serving their readers.

Another difficulty is staff. Many libraries cannot obtain or keep the staff they require. This applies to junior as well as senior staff. Libraries offer interesting work, but pay only average wages, and ask their staff to be on duty in the evenings and on Saturdays.

A third difficulty stems from the number of library users, particularly student users, which has been increasing in recent years at a tremendous rate. This has put the services libraries offer under ever-mounting pressure; it is hard for services under pressure to keep up a consistently high standard.

This discussion of standards of service must not end without some indication of what constitutes a reasonable standard. Is it in fact possible to measure the standard of service offered by a library? In the autumn 1969 issue of *What* there appeared an article called *How to test your library*. This article revealed the results of judging thirty-eight public libraries on a points system, points being awarded for such measures of service as hours of opening and proportion of qualified staff. The maximum number of points that could be scored was fourteen, and the ratings varied from thirteen down to four. The article was a pioneer attempt to assess both the range and the quality of services offered by public libraries, and, as can be seen from the variation in the number of points awarded, considerable differences in standards were found to exist. The survey was limited in too many ways for its results to be altogether valid. Nevertheless, the article is well worth reading.

A method anyone can use to gauge standards of service in a library is now put forward. It suggests five basic hallmarks of a good library, all of which should be easily ascertained when looked for. They are:

(i) The library is tidy. The books are kept in reasonable order on the shelves, the condition of the stock is fair (for example, books wanting rebinding have been rebound) and the overall impression is that the library is looked after.

(ii) The rules of the library are made public. They are kept – but in spirit rather than to the last letter.

(iii) The services offered are sufficient to allow the library to be used without any feelings of frustration. All services are advertised and the staff encourage you to make use of the services.

(iv) The library is well guided. There are enough signposts to enable you to find your way around easily. There are signposts to departments, to subjects, and to shelves. In addition, the guiding is up to date.

(v) Staff assistance is available, and this assistance is courteous and informed. The staff are prepared, if necessary, to help you find and do things, not just to tell you where to go and what to do.

BOOKS FOR FURTHER STUDY

CENTRAL YOUTH EMPLOYMENT EXECUTIVE. *Librarianship, Information and Archive Work.* 7th ed. HMSO. 1968. (Choice of Careers Series, no. 4.)

CHANDLER, G. *Libraries in the Modern World.* Pergamon, 1965.

HARRISON, K. C. *Libraries in Britain.* Longmans, 1968.

What (National Suggestions Centre Ltd), Autumn, 1969.

Chapter 2
The services libraries offer

Many services that libraries offer their readers have been touched upon in the previous chapter. However, in view of the aims of this book, they need to be considered thoroughly and systematically. The services that libraries offer will now be considered under twenty-one headings; the number immediately indicates the wide range of services that can be offered. Public libraries probably offer the greatest variety of services and so are used as the basis of this chapter.

I. STAFF ASSISTANCE

This service is placed first because it is the most important. The trained librarian, it is said, should know where the answer to every question can be found. There is a touch of exaggeration to that statement but there is no doubt that the assistance of a member of the library staff can save time and prevent frustration. Many libraries have a senior member of their staff at an enquiry desk, and this is the member of the staff whose assistance should be sought. If there is no enquiry desk, the staff at the main library counter or control point should be approached. There are four main types of problems that readers seem to have. They want advice on choosing books; they want information on books; they want to be guided round the library; they require information on a particular subject. The staff are capable of solving all these problems. Readers who are not able to visit the library are normally able to obtain staff assistance by writing or telephoning. They may even be able to call the library on telex. On subjects other than those directly connected with books, the library staff will not generally give advice, though a few public libraries have a specially trained staff who run a Citizens' Advice Bureau. In a

number of places the librarian is also the official local government information and publicity officer.

The amount of staff assistance that can be obtained varies
from library to library, and is undoubtedly greatest in libraries
of industrial firms. This is because the ratio of staff to library
users here is high, and also because it has been found generally
more efficient for librarians to do library research than for the
scientists and managers to do it for themselves.

2. TRAINING OF READERS

Quite apart from giving readers staff assistance when they
request it, some libraries, mainly academic ones, offer formal
training in the use of the library. This is an excellent idea, not
just because it makes for more efficient use but because many
readers are reluctant to approach staff members with their
problems. A course of formal training makes them more ready
to approach staff and at the same time more independent, as
by the end of the course they can solve many of their library
problems for themselves. The training of readers is accom-
plished in a number of ways, including the use of close-circuit
television and films. Often, it is no more than an introduction
to the library, what it offers, and how it is arranged. It may,
however, include a study of reference books and other valuable
sources of information.

3. BOOKS TO TAKE HOME

The lending departments of public libraries are usually open
every morning and afternoon except Sunday, and on Monday
to Friday evenings, though the actual times will vary depending on the size and location of the library. The large urban
libraries have the longest opening hours, particularly those that
are divided into subject departments, for such departments
combine lending with reference functions. The opening hours
of non-public libraries will be very varied. Some, like those in
schools, will close during the holidays, while others, like those in
universities and colleges, will shorten their opening hours at
such times. Both public and non-public libraries may lend
books by post. Indeed, in the early days of county libraries,

people like farmers who lived in isolated places had no alternative way of using their public library. Now, however, mobile libraries are the rule in rural areas, and isolated farms and cottages receive a personal visit from the library van.

The borrowing of books is usually restricted to registered members of the library. In most non-public libraries only members of the firm, school, etc., can borrow books. In public libraries, membership will be open to all, but readers residing outside the town or county providing the library may have to pay a subscription. Public libraries are sometimes termed free libraries as no subscription is otherwise charged. This term is inaccurate as the local ratepayer contributes towards the cost of the library service every time he pays his rates.

Borrowers may be allowed to take out as many books as they wish, but most libraries limit the number that any person may have at any one time. It is usually possible to borrow a reasonable number, and in fact extra 'tickets' may be available on request. In the last few years methods of issuing books, especially in public libraries, have become more mechanized, and these new methods commonly do away with readers having a limited number of tickets. Instead the reader is issued with a membership card which he must present whenever he wants to borrow a book.

When a library has several branches or departments it is customary to allow members to borrow books not only from the service point at which they joined, but from the other service points as well, returning each book to the service point from which it was taken. To help people return books, a few libraries have a sort of 'night safe', where readers can deposit them after the library has closed.

The usual period of loan in public libraries is fourteen days, and books in great demand may only be loaned for a week. However, it is nearly always possible to renew books not in demand for a further period. This may be done by post and phone as well as in person. A few large public libraries even have automatic telephone renewal equipment. Longer periods of loan are common in non-public libraries, and such libraries may also loan out reference books overnight. An increasing number of public libraries are loaning at least some of their books for three weeks or a month, and students may be able to borrow books for even longer periods. At holiday times it may be possible to take out books for the length of the holiday. However, many borrowers avail themselves of another service at such times. By showing the library at their holiday resort proof that they are members of their local public library, they are entitled to borrow books for the length of their holiday. Many public libraries not situated in holiday resorts also allow outside readers to borrow books on the same conditions.

It might be mentioned at this point that the rules libraries lay down governing the use of their services are made so as to keep those services running as smoothly as possible. It is annoying to find, for example, that fines have to be paid on books that have been kept out too long, but the object of fines is not unreasonable; it is to stop books lying idle and forgotten.

Some libraries allow readers to borrow not only single copies of books but also sets of plays, musical scores and textbooks. School and college libraries may have sets of all these three kinds of material, public libraries just sets of plays and musical scores. The normal practice is for a responsible member of the drama group or musical society to borrow the sets on behalf of the society. The lending of sets of plays and musical scores is closely related to the next service to be described.

4. OTHER MATERIAL FOR BORROWING

Some libraries allow readers to take home periodicals, holiday guides and other pamphlet material, gramophone records, tape recordings, films, film strips, slides, illustrations, even paintings and pottery. This is because libraries are the most obvious source of supply of most of these materials, even though many of them do not physically resemble books. Visual aids, such as film strips, are an essential part of the stock of school and college libraries, whilst the libraries belonging to industrial firms spend a great deal of effort in sending members of the firm the periodicals of value to them in their work. The number of public libraries supplying some of these additional materials for borrowing is increasing. Readers who use them may, however, have to contribute towards their cost.

In the future, this aspect of library service will surely expand. Many American public libraries have, indeed, had separate audio-visual departments for years, and these lend films and recordings. And now the coming of videotapes and related methods of using one's own television receiver mean that the range and possibilities of audio-visual materials is increasing all the time. In a few years, perhaps, borrowers of television programmes will be as common in libraries as book borrowers are now.

5. FACILITIES FOR STUDY

There may be no facilities for study in small public library branches, but most libraries offer some of those that will now be mentioned. There may only be a few tables situated at one end of the lending library, around which the library's few reference books will be shelved. But in many libraries the study tables will be in a separate room probably called the reference library or study room. There may be even small private study rooms, commonly called carrels, where readers doing prolonged research can work in total quiet. A few libraries have sound-proof rooms or hoods where students can use typewriters and tape recorders (which incidentally are not normally supplied by the library). All libraries should also have a magnifying glass as the print in some reference books, and particularly on some maps, can be very difficult to read. It is usually possible to use the study facilities of libraries even when only working with one's own books and not with library materials.

6. BOOKS FOR REFERENCE

Reference books can be used either as sources of information or for the purpose of study. Most people prefer to read books at home, but there are good reasons why the following three kinds of books are available for use only in libraries. The first kind of reference book is the quick-reference book. The main reason why encyclopaedias, dictionaries, and similar works are not for loan is that they are designed merely to be referred to. If they are always available in the library they can be referred to by many people over a short period of time. The second kind of reference book is either a standard work or a monograph. This kind of book is available for reference so that readers doing

study or research in the library can see at any time the books
they require. Copies of reference books of this second kind
should be available for lending whenever possible. The third
kind of reference book is the rare book. Old and valuable books
are often for reference only because they are irreplaceable.
Many reference libraries, incidentally, include collections of
such books given to the library by local book-collectors.

7. SUPPLEMENTARY REFERENCE MATERIAL

Newspapers and periodicals, newspaper and periodical clippings, pamphlets, manuscripts, maps, sheet music, illustrations,
microtexts; these eight types of material mentioned in Chapter 3
under 'The arrangement of other library materials' are all
supplementary reference materials. However, this material can
be grouped in another way, depending on the particular
information it provides. Trade catalogues, produced by firms
to describe their products, and patent specifications, which
describe the latest inventions, are such groups. Many other
service groups exist each of which contains pamphlets,
periodicals, and possibly also books, but it will be sufficient
to note just three. They are government publications, standard
specifications, and company information.

The publications of the British government, let alone those
of other governments, are themselves so numerous and complicated that large reference libraries have specially trained
members of staff to deal with them. Some government publications, such as Acts of Parliament, are directly concerned with
Parliament, but most government publications are so called
because they are produced by departments of the central
government. Examples of such publications are those produced
by the Department of Education and Science to aid and advise
teachers. Large reference libraries often take all British
government publications.

Standard specifications, as the name suggests, are those publications that lay down standards stating exactly how a product
should be made, or what security precautions should be taken.
The majority are issued by the British Standards Institution;
they should be found in all libraries with a reasonable collection
of technical books.

Company information, to turn from a technical to a commercial subject, is another group of material much in demand. Information concerning public companies will generally be available in libraries, as information about such companies is easily found, for example, in the standard quick reference book, *The Stock Exchange Yearbook*. The financial details of smaller firms are not published in the same way but some libraries will have a little helpful information on them.

8. REQUESTS AND RESERVATIONS

When a book or other item is not in stock, it is usually possible to request that it be added. In non-public libraries readers have a greater say in what material is ordered for the library than in public libraries. However, all libraries pay attention to requests from their readers. Usually the reader fills in a request form and then is notified when the work has been added to the library.

Books that are in stock and for loan can also be reserved if they are out when a new reader wants them. A reservation automatically results in the required book being put on one side immediately it is next returned to the library. The reader who has made the reservation is notified that the book awaits him. He must then come and collect it within the few days given him. A small charge is made by most public libraries for reservations.

In reference libraries, especially the national libraries, a reservation system of a rather different sort is available. Readers who will be visiting the library on a particular day can write in a few days beforehand and have the material they want to consult made ready for them to use.

9. INTER-LIBRARY LOANS

When a reader makes a reservation he may not know whether the book he requires is in stock or not. After all, many libraries have a number of branches, and what may not be in stock at one service point may well be available at another. The reader is sometimes asked at the time he makes the reservation if he is prepared to have the work borrowed from another library for him if it is not at any service point of his own library. (Incidentally, it should be noted that some reservations are satisfied by the library ordering the reserved item when they find that it is not already in their stock.) He is asked because inter-library lending may take longer, because occasionally a book borrowed from another library can be marked 'For use only in the library', and because there may be an inter-lending charge levied by the library.

Inter-library loans have been part of the service offered by British libraries for many years, as they have for a long time realized that they need to co-operate with each other in order to satisfy their readers. In addition to borrowing from nearby libraries, libraries borrow from further afield. They do so as members of Regional Library Bureaux, and it is to these bureaux therefore that they send their inter-loan applications. Regional bureaux are organizations set up by libraries to control the lending of books, etc., from one library to another. There are nine such bureaux and each one is responsible for a particular area of Great Britain (for example, the bureau housed in the Central Public Library at Leicester is responsible for the East Midlands). If the book is anywhere within the region, the bureau will trace its location and have it sent to the library making the request. If the book cannot be traced within the region, then the request will normally be sent to the National Central Library in London. This library is the national centre for inter-library lending. If the National Central Library discovers there is no copy of the book in this country at all, then it may endeavour to satisfy the request from abroad, and hundreds of books each year are lent to and borrowed from foreign libraries.

To improve the system that has been described above, many libraries in recent years have agreed to specialize in particular subjects, purchasing virtually all new books on those subjects. Today, therefore, libraries are increasingly able to satisfy demands even for obscure and specialized publications.

In addition to the scheme of inter-lending outlined above, there is one other of outstanding importance. It is the one organized by the National Lending Library for Science and Technology, and it is organized on quite a different basis from the Regional Bureaux-National Central Library scheme.

The National Lending Library does all the lending, acting as a sort of warehouse. Books and periodicals in science and technology, together with social science periodicals, are those within its scope. Member libraries pay for each item they borrow, but the cost is very reasonable and the service speedy. Special libraries have been particularly helped by the National Lending Library scheme, as they are often in need of unusual periodical articles, and want them in a hurry. A valuable feature of the scheme is that it is possible to obtain a photocopy instead of the item itself. It costs a little more, but you do not have to return a photocopy, and so it remains handy for future use.

10. PHOTOCOPYING

All large reference libraries, and many libraries of other kinds, offer facilities for copying photographically material they have in stock. The greatest demand is usually for periodical articles. Libraries will also obtain for readers photocopies of material not in their stock from other libraries. When a photocopying service is offered certain conditions governing its use have to be observed, for otherwise the law of copyright – that is, the sole right to produce or reproduce a book, etc. – would be broken. The reader will be asked to pay the cost of copying, he will only be allowed a single copy, and he must sign that the copy is for his personal use. It may be necessary for the reader to obtain the permission of the owner of the copyright before the copy can be made.

Photocopying equipment is developing all the time, and whilst in the past photocopies in most libraries had to be requested a day or two before they were required, on-the-spot photocopying is now the rule. The cost of photocopies varies but copying illustrations is usually more expensive than copying text matter. Copies of a page of text matter should not cost more than 5p, though if you are using a self-service machine, which a number of libraries have installed, you may have to pay more.

In addition to the copying of periodical articles and extracts from books, libraries, especially those of universities, make transparencies for various kinds of projectors.

11. TRANSLATIONS

In the larger libraries belonging to industrial firms, there will always be facilities for readers to have documents translated. This service is also provided by a few other libraries. However, most public libraries will only suggest a person or organization who will translate the document for the reader, though it should be remembered that they will have available for reference a selection of translating dictionaries.

12. PREPARING PERSONAL BIBLIOGRAPHIES AND READING LISTS

Bibliographies are compiled by libraries of all kinds, but particularly by the staff of special libraries. It is obviously an invaluable service for the reader who requires a list of books, periodical articles and other material on the subject he is studying. The subjects of such bibliographies are usually highly specialized, though the references in them may be limited to the stock of the compiling library.

Reading lists are less specialized compilations, prepared to help a particular reader develop his reading interests. Such a service, which is akin to the giving of advice on the choice of books, is uncommon in British public libraries, but is an established feature of Russian ones.

13. CIRCULATING MATERIAL AND INFORMATION

All kinds of libraries circulate material and information. Sometimes it is done at the request of readers, but usually readers and potential readers are circularized by the library. It has already been mentioned that the libraries of industrial firms circulate periodicals. They may similarly circulate summaries, commonly called abstracts, of the contents of periodical articles. In some libraries the information will take the form of an index to recent periodical articles, arranged by subject. Libraries also circulate publicity material. For example, a large public library with a technical department may circulate all the local firms with a pamphlet describing the information it can offer on the subject of patents. Libraries of all kinds sometimes find out their readers' requirements and interests, and then notify them when they receive new material they think will be of value to them. This last service is also done informally when library staff personally tell readers news that they feel the readers ought to know.

14. PUBLICATIONS

The main types of library publications helpful to readers are three in number: book-lists and bulletins; bibliographies and catalogues; guides to the library and its resources.

Book-lists are most often of recent additions to stock, whilst library bulletins (or magazines) usually include such a list. However, many libraries issue lists of books available on particular subjects, such as Photography, or Collecting Antiques. Incidentally, the information other than book-lists to be found in library bulletins varies from notes of other library news to scholarly articles on books, literature and local history.

Bibliographies and catalogues are usually rather more ambitious publications and so are met with less frequently. However, the development of computers has led to a number of libraries being able to produce a regularly updated catalogue in the form of a computer print-out.

Guides to a library and its resources may be general in scope or devoted to a particular aspect of the library. Only a few libraries have produced for the use of their readers detailed handbooks, but a good number have issued booklets containing the most important information. These booklets sometimes form a series, each one describing a different service or department of the library. These more specialized guides are also a feature of many library bulletins.

15. INDEXES

In a large number of libraries the staff compile certain indexes in order that the resources of the library may be more fully brought out, and that readers' enquiries may be better satisfied. For example a municipal public library may compile an index to the town's newspaper (this is particularly valuable to local history students), and have a card index of information that it knows is not readily available in any other place. Such indexes are invaluable and occasionally there is even a demand for them to be published, but, generally speaking, publication is not appropriate as their primary purpose is to serve the particular library's need.

Special libraries also compile indexes, especially indexes of periodical articles of interest to their line of business. The compilation of all kinds of indexes is related to the techniques of classification and cataloguing, which are dealt with in the next chapter.

16. AID TO SOCIETIES

These next four services mainly concern public libraries. Libraries assist societies and other mainly local organizations in various ways. They allow the society to deposit its collection of books with them, they loan books out to the society, they compile lists of books of interest to society members, they permit the society to hold exhibitions in the library, they encourage the society to meet in the library, they talk about the library to the society. Libraries also often display books at local shows and other exhibitions.

17. AID TO SCHOOLS

Libraries and schools co-operate in a number of ways. The co-operation is usually greatest in county libraries, as the county education committee often controls the libraries as well as the schools. The co-operation varies from virtually full control of the school libraries by the county libraries to asking head-teachers to vouch for children who want to join the public library. Libraries may loan books to schools, display books for them, and in many other ways help teachers to run their school libraries. They may talk to school children on the use of books and libraries, they may organize exhibitions and competitions of interest to them.

18. AID TO HANDICAPPED READERS

Such groups as hospital patients, the blind, the aged, and those in prison are aided by libraries in various ways. Libraries send books to hospitals, old peoples' homes, and to prisons.

They help the blind to obtain their special kinds of books, and they run door to door book services for 'shut-ins'.

19. AID TO OTHER SPECIAL GROUPS

Two other special groups worthy of mention are local councillors and local firms. A number of public libraries offer special services to their councillors, such as the provision of a collection of books near the Council Chamber, and the circulation of lists of recent articles on local government. Firms in the library's area are catered for in a variety of ways. In many large towns the public library organizes a scheme of library co-operation between itself and the libraries of local firms. The first of these schemes, the Sheffield one, was started as long ago as 1933, but most of them are comparatively new. Many of the schemes include, as well as the inter-lending of books, the production of a bulletin, special photocopying facilities, and perhaps a translations service.

20. ADULT EDUCATION ACTIVITIES

As well as helping societies, many of which are concerned with adult education in some form, libraries carry out their own adult education activities, acting indeed as the cultural centre of the community. They have classes and more informal educational groups, they run concerts, exhibitions, lectures, and film shows. Some librarians are responsible for museums and art galleries, occasionally even for theatres. Where this is so, there will obviously be close links between these and the library.

With the coming of the Open University, public libraries will become even more closely linked with adult education. They will not only stock the textbooks and other reading needed by this university's students, they will become centres where the students can meet to view and discuss appropriate radio and television programmes.

21. SUPPLEMENTARY FACILITIES

This heading is used to cover services not connected with books, but all the same provided, at least in large library buildings. Supplementary facilities offered by libraries include car and cycle parks, coffee and snack bars, washing and toilet facilities, coat and baggage racks. One public library, Haringey, has made available a room where parents may leave toddlers while they choose their books.

These are the services libraries offer. To ensure that as many readers as possible are familiar with what is offered them, libraries utilize nearly every form of publicity. As well as publishing guides they offer talks, organize exhibitions, and conduct tours round the library. Though no single library is likely to offer all the services outlined, the libraries you use will offer many of them.

If you are in doubt at all as to what services your library offers, then find out. Study any guides published by your library, and ask the staff for further information. If you think your library should provide some service which it does not appear to provide at the moment, broach the idea of such a service. It may well be that the librarian has only been waiting for some positive demand from his readers before offering that very service.

BOOKS FOR FURTHER STUDY

COLLISON, R. L. *Library Assistance to Readers*. 5th ed. Crosby Lockwood, 1965.

FOSKETT, D. J. *Information Service in Libraries*. 2nd ed. Crosby Lockwood, 1967.

Chapter 3
How libraries are arranged

When a reader has found his way into the library he wants to use or, in the case of a large library, into the department he wants to use, he has then to find his way round it. Most of the space will be taken up by books, and those books will be arranged in some sort of order. Generally speaking, there will be one main sequence of books, lending or reference, depending on whether the library is a lending or a reference library. In a lending library, however, there will be a small separate sequence of quick-reference books. These, which consist mainly of dictionaries, encyclopaedias, yearbooks, and similar works, enable answers to be found speedily on a wide range of subjects. In libraries such as the subject departments of the large public libraries, where the stock consists of both lending and reference books, the two are sometimes placed side by side in one sequence. The advantage of this is that the resources of the department can be seen at a glance, all the books on any topic being together. The disadvantage of the system, as may be imagined, is that though the reference books are distinguished in some way from the lending books, a large number of readers still try to borrow them.

In many libraries there are several small sequences of books in addition to the main sequence. There is often a sequence of oversize books, that is, books which are too big to fit on ordinary bookshelves. Many of the library's art books and musical scores will be found in the oversize sequence. When there is a foreign literature collection, this will usually be shelved in a separate sequence. There is also, in some libraries, a special collection of books. This may be shelved separately because it is a collection donated to the library. The Pepys Collection in the library of Magdalene College, Cambridge, is an example of this kind of special collection. It may be shelved separately because it covers a particular topic in great detail, the collection dealing, perhaps, with the history of the locality, or with the principal industry of the area, or with a literary figure. Where the library has collections of library materials other than books, these will also be arranged usually in separate sequences. The arrangement of these materials is considered at the end of this chapter.

The arrangement of books

Books are mostly arranged under subject, so that readers can find all the travel books, all the books on engineering, or whatever they want, together on the shelves. Fiction books may also be arranged by subject, e.g. Westerns, Romances, Science Fiction, but are often in a single alphabetical sequence under authors' names. In a small library the arrangement of the non-fiction books by subject might be carried out very simply. The librarian would think of about a dozen subject headings, such as Science, Literature, History, and would then arrange these headings in alphabetical order round the library. He would allocate his books to these headings, probably placing some sort of symbol on the books to show which heading they were to be shelved under. Within each subject heading the books would be arranged alphabetically under the names of the authors. This simple method of arranging books is commonly used in bookshops. However, in most libraries it is felt that the books need to be arranged not just under a broad subject heading, such as Science, but under the precise subject that they are about – atomic physics, calculus, the moon, or whatever it may be. Arranging books under their precise subject is not always easy, and therefore most libraries use one of several published classification schemes for books. These are so called because they enable all the books on any particular subject to be placed together on the shelves. At the same time, they allow for books on related topics to be shelved nearby. For example, near the place for the subject of arithmetic, there will be places for the books on algebra, geometry and mathematics generally. This classified arrangement under subject, as it is called, enables readers not only to see what the library has on any particular subject, but, without searching, reveals what it has on related subjects. Within any particular subject heading the books are normally arranged in alphabetical order of author.

At this point one or two remarks on the principle of classification are called for. Classification is the art of arranging any group of objects so that those which have something in common are placed together. As a result, of course, those which have nothing in common will be separated from one another. Classification plays a considerable part in everyday life. The mind is always classifying: buildings seen, people met, sounds heard; the classification of books works on the same principles. Book classification schemes, however, have some distinctive features. The most important of these is the shorthand symbol they attach to every subject they list. The purpose of this symbol, usually called the class number or the notation, is to stand for the subject of the book. It takes the form, in the main, of letters or numbers. It is designed to be conveniently placed on all the lists of the books in the library, and just as conveniently marked on the books themselves. It is always to be found on the spine of the book, which is the part that can be seen when the book is on the shelf. The notation also reveals the place of any particular subject within the scheme.

The most popular book classification scheme is the one invented by the American librarian, Melvil Dewey, and first published in 1876. This scheme, often referred to as the Dewey Decimal Classification scheme, will be considered in detail. It should be noted, however, that there are a number of other important classification schemes, such as the Library of Congress's own scheme.

As well as general classification schemes, there are also many designed for the classification of individual subjects, such as local history. An example is the scheme devised by the British Rubber Manufacturers' Research Association for use in libraries specializing in material about rubber. Special classification schemes, catering not for a subject but for a type of reader, also exist. The School Library Association has, for example, adapted the Decimal Classification for schoolchildren. The title of the adaptation is *Introduction to the Dewey Decimal Classification for British Schools* (2nd ed. 1968).

Though virtually all libraries use one of the classification schemes mentioned, there are a few who have built up their own. The scheme used by the University of Bristol library is an example of the home-made variety. Many libraries, however, have made alterations to the scheme that they use, so as to make it better suit their needs. But in the last few years the tendency has been towards uniformity of practice. The main reason for this swing has been the publication since 1950 of the *British National Bibliography*. This work, of which more will be said later, classifies by the Dewey Decimal Classification every book received, under the law of legal deposit, at the British Museum. Published weekly, and in collected form at longer intervals, it can be bought by any library. As a result many libraries are content to let it do their classification for them, at least in part.

THE DEWEY DECIMAL CLASSIFICATION

This scheme has now reached its eighteenth edition (1971). Compared with the thirty-six pages of the first edition, the eighteenth runs to three volumes. The examples given in this book are from this edition. There is also an abridged version of the scheme, designed for small libraries; this has now reached its tenth edition (1972). The popularity of this scheme, now admitted to have many faults, is mainly due to its having been the best scheme available at the time when the majority of libraries were establishing themselves.

The scheme first divides the knowledge contained in books into ten parts or classes. The notation of the scheme consists solely of numbers, and every book must be represented by at least a three-figure number. The ten main classes with their class numbers are:

Generalities	000
Philosophy and related disciplines	100
Religion	200
The Social Sciences	300
Language	400
Pure Sciences	500
Technology	600
The Arts	700
Literature and rhetoric	800
History, General Geography, etc.	900

The scheme then divides each of the main classes into ten, and allows this division by ten to be repeated as often as is necessary to give each individual subject a place in the scheme. If the main class, Pure Sciences (500) is examined, it will be seen that its ten divisions are:

General works on pure science	500
Mathematics	510
Astronomy and allied sciences	520
Physics	530
Chemistry and allied sciences	540
Earth sciences	550
Palaeontology	560
Anthropological and biological sciences	570
Botanical sciences	580
Zoological sciences	590

If the subject Mathematics (510) is divided in its turn, the divisions revealed are:

General works on mathematics	510–11
Algebra	512
Arithmetic	513
Topology	514
Analysis	515
Geometry	516
(Left blank)	517–18
Probabilities and statistical mathematics	519

Although the system allows always for subjects to be split into ten parts, when ten parts cannot be found certain class numbers are not allocated a subject, as 517–18 above. If future discoveries reveal the existence of new subjects, and such discoveries have been common in the last few years in the fields of science and technology, then such numbers can be allocated one of these new subjects.

It is partly because the system allows for every subject to be divided into ten that it is known as the Decimal Classification. Another reason, however, is that the notation requires a decimal point to be placed after the third figure. In other words, if the subject of Arithmetic (513), for example, is divided up the class numbers resulting will not only be four figures in length, but will include a decimal point after the third figure.

General books on arithmetic	513
Numeration systems	513·1
Fundamental operations	513·2
Prime numbers and factoring	513·3
Fractions and decimal fractions etc.	513·4

The class numbers of all the subjects most likely to be required by readers are given in the Appendix at the back of this book.

Some more details remain to be given about the scheme. These are to do with the way it deals with subjects that, for various reasons, do not fit into the normal arrangement of the scheme. It has been shown that the scheme divides up books by placing them on the shelves under the subject they are about. But some books, such as encyclopaedias, are not about any particular subject, and in other books the subject matter is less important to the reader than the literary form in which the subject is presented, in the form of a novel for example, or in the form of a play. The scheme deals with encyclopaedias and similar works by placing them in the first main class, Generalities (000). Books in which the subject is of less importance than the form in which it is presented are placed in the Literature class (800) which is divided not by subject, but by language and then by form. For example, the forms listed under the English Literature division (820) are:

English poetry	821
English drama	822
English fiction	823
English essays	824
English speeches	825
English letters	826
English satire and humour	827
English miscellany	828

The class number 829 is not allocated to a form of literature but to Old English (Anglo-Saxon) Literature. The literature of other languages is divided in a similar way. In most libraries though, English fiction is not shelved at 823 but in a separate sequence, arranged alphabetically by author.

No more need be said about the Dewey Decimal Classification as a whole, but some more information about its notation is called for. The notation is so designed that if the number representing a certain subject is known, it may be of help when searching for books on a seemingly quite different subject. Two ways in which it may help are therefore illustrated. The first concerns the class numbers standing for the history of countries. For example, the number for English History is 942. Now a book dealing with English Education will be given the number 370.942, a book on English Politics the number 320.942, a book on English Architecture the number 720.942. In other words, though the general subject number is obviously different, in each case the same additional number (942) is added to represent the locality 'England', and this is none other than the number that by itself stands for English History. The second concerns books that deal with their subject matter in a particular way. For example, a book on the history of a subject is given, in addition to its general subject number, an additional symbol (09) which represents history. This symbol should not be confused with the locality numbers that can be added, such as 942. The same history number can be added, no matter what the subject is. A book on the history of Sport will have the number 796.09, on the history of Arithmetic the number 513.09, on the history of the Theatre 792.09. Note that if the subject number already has a 'o' at the end of it, for example 510 (Mathematics), the figure '9' only is added as, for example, history of Mathematics 510.9.

There are nine main symbols that can be used in this way. They are:

Philosophy and theory	01
Miscellany	02
Dictionaries, Encyclopaedias, Concordances	03
(Left blank)	04
Serial publications	05
Organizations	06
Study and teaching	07
Collections and anthologies	08
History and geographical treatment	09

Having considered the classification of books, it is obvious that readers, if they know the class number of the subject they are seeking, should be able to find the books they want on the shelves. But very often the reader will not know or have any idea of the class number. What is he to do then? Two possibilities are open to him. The first one is for him to find the books he wants by looking at the guides to the class numbers displayed by the library. These guides should be provided above every bookcase, and should contain not only the names of the subjects on those shelves, but also the class numbers of those subjects. *Shelf guides* is the general name given to these guides in libraries. They are very useful, but a few words of caution

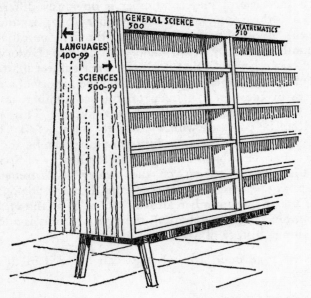

1. Shelf guides

must be given on the use of them. Though shelf guides can be provided for every important subject, they of course cannot list every subject on which the library has books. Do not, therefore, be surprised if the name of the subject you are seeking is not listed. You should be able to find the place you want by looking for the appropriate more general subject heading. But there are pitfalls. The Decimal Classification places books on Insurance, for example, under Social Services, and gives them the class number 368. There may be no shelf guide listing the subject, though there should be one listing the more general subject of Social Services. However, few readers would look under Social Services for books on Insurance; most would look under the section of the shelves headed Commerce. This section would be nowhere near that on Social Services. When using shelf guides it is also necessary to remember that libraries are constantly buying new books and discarding old ones, and that the position of any one book on their shelves will not remain constant. Shelf guides are usually moveable, but they cannot always indicate slight changes in the place of books. So if you cannot find the books you want where it seems they ought to be, try the shelves above and below.

The second possibility open to the reader who does not know where to locate books on the subject he wants is to consult the catalogue. This is, indeed, the sure way of locating a subject.

The catalogue

To librarians the classification and cataloguing of a book go together, both processes usually being done by the same person at the same time. If a book were only classified it would always be in its right position on the library shelves, but it could only be found by readers knowing the class number of the book. One of the purposes of the catalogue is to provide a key to the class numbers of books, so that readers can look under the name of the subject in the catalogue and find its class number. Another purpose of the catalogue is to provide a record of all the books in the library, so that a reader knowing the author or title of a book can find out if the library has that particular book. A third purpose is to provide a complete list of all the books that the library contains, subject by subject. This is important, for in no library at any one time is every book on the shelves. In lending libraries many books are on loan to readers, and even in reference libraries there are books being used by other readers. Other reasons why books can be missing from the shelves are that they may be being repaired; they may be shelved in reserve; they may belong to a special collection shelved elsewhere.

The catalogue does serve certain other purposes. As well as giving the class number, the author, and the title of each book, it gives further details about the book, such as the number of pages, details of the illustrations, and the date of publication. This information is particularly valuable to readers who want to find the books on a subject that will be most useful to them, and who are using a large reference library which keeps most of its stock in reserve.

There are five physical forms that the catalogue may take. It may be like any other book, this type being known as a printed catalogue. It may be a series of loose-leaf binders, each containing slips giving details of books. This type is known as a sheaf catalogue. It may be in a cabinet, with the details of the books on small cards that fit into drawers. This type of catalogue is known as the card catalogue, and as it is the most popular type, the information given in the rest of this section will particularly relate to this type. The fourth type of catalogue takes the form of a visible index. This will usually consist of a series of metal frames fixed to a wall and holding slips of paper or card on which the details of the books are given. The final type of catalogue is the computer catalogue. Catalogue information is stored in a computer and printed out as required.

HOW CATALOGUES ARE ARRANGED

The drawers of a card catalogue look at first rather forbidding, but there should be on top of the cabinet instructions on how to use the catalogue, and on the front of each drawer a brief note of its contents. The contents of the drawers will also have guide cards inserted amongst them. If the contents form a single alphabetical sequence the catalogue is what librarians call a Dictionary Catalogue. It is obvious how this name has been acquired, as the type of books called dictionaries are also arranged in a single alphabetical sequence. A Dictionary Catalogue includes a card for each book under the name of the author, and another under the name of the subject. For example, E. L. Woodward's *History of England* would be given a card under Woodward and another under ENGLAND, HISTORY. A book will always be indexed under both author and subject, and often the catalogue will contain more than two cards representing the book. A book may have more than one author, and if so an additional card will be added for

each additional author. Or a card may be added under the
title of the book. If the title of the book describes the subject
of the book, as with the book by Woodward, *A History of
England*, an additional card is not placed under the title; but
if it does not, as with the book by Gavin Maxwell called *A Reed*

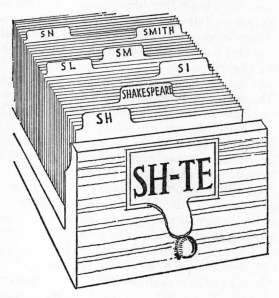

2. A card catalogue drawer

Shaken by the Wind (the subject of which is travel in Iraq), a card
is placed under the title.

More common than the Dictionary Catalogue in this country
is the Classified Catalogue with its three sequences of cards.
It is so called because the principal sequence is arranged in
classified order. The three sequences consist of an alphabetical
sequence of cards under authors' names, a second sequence
arranged in the same way as the books on the shelves, that is in
the order of the classification scheme used by the library, and a
sequence that gives in alphabetical order the names of subjects
followed by the class number for those subjects. This third
sequence does not give details of individual books. The first
sequence is known as the author catalogue. However, as it
often contains cards under the names of people written about,

as in biographies and literary studies, some libraries use the term name catalogue for this sequence. Cards placed under the titles of books will be included in the author catalogue unless the library has a separate title catalogue. The second sequence is known as the classified catalogue. The third sequence is the subject index. Sometimes the subject index cards do not form a separate sequence, but are inserted in the author catalogue. In a few libraries there is no subject index; instead readers have the use of a copy of the index to the classification scheme used by the library.

There has always been controversy between librarians as to which is the better of these two kinds of catalogue, the Dictionary Catalogue or the Classified Catalogue. The Dictionary Catalogue is obviously easier to understand; its main snags are to do with the cards filed under the name of the subject of the book. The book by Woodward, previously mentioned, will fairly obviously go under the subject heading, ENGLAND, HISTORY, but what about the book by A. W. Judge on *Automobile Engine Overhaul*? Should this be placed under the heading AUTOMOBILES, or should the heading be labelled VEHICLES, or MOTOR-CARS or just CARS? It can be seen that finding the right subject heading is not always easy, though if the wrong heading is looked up, there should be directions indicating where to look. Even subject headings such as ENGLAND, HISTORY are not straightforward. The word that most precisely classifies the subject of the book in this case is ENGLAND, as the word history only indicates how the subject is dealt with. And so, the heading chosen is not HISTORY OF ENGLAND but ENGLAND, HISTORY. It will be found that many subject headings are inverted in this way. Another snag awaits readers looking for books on all aspects of a particular subject, for example GARDENING. All books on gardening are near each other on the shelves, but in a Dictionary Catalogue the subject cards representing those books will not all be under the subject heading GARDENING. There would be far too many cards for readers to wade through if the cards were placed under comparatively broad subject headings such as GARDENING, so libraries place them under the most precise subject headings possible. The general books on gardening would be placed under the heading GARDENING, but the books on particular aspects of gardening under the names of those aspects, e.g. ROSES. So the reader looking for books on various aspects of gardening has to go from place to place in the drawers to satisfy his requirements.

The main snag with the Classified Catalogue is that before the reader can discover what books the library has on any particular subject, he must first consult the subject index and note the number under which to look in the classified sequence. For example, to find the books on ENGLAND, HISTORY it is necessary first to consult the index under that heading. This would reveal a card made out as shown below.

ENGLAND, HISTORY 942

It might seem that if a reader knows what he wants and knows what kind of a catalogue he is dealing with, he will have little difficulty in finding the information he requires. Most catalogue sequences are arranged in alphabetical order, and nothing seems simpler than this arrangement. But with any catalogue, and especially with a large dictionary catalogue, the vast number of cards contained in it makes for complexities. The first point the reader should note is whether the arrangement of the alphabetical sequence is 'letter by letter' or 'word by word'. These two terms need explaining. If a list of words, for example a list of place names, is examined closely, it can be seen that two sorts of alphabetical arrangement are possible. The result of arranging the words Eastbourne, Eccles, East Ham, East Grinstead, Eastleigh, Ealing, and East Lothian in the two ways is given below.

Letter by letter	*Word by word*
Ealing	Ealing
Eastbourne	East Grinstead
East Grinstead	East Ham
East Ham	East Lothian
Eastleigh	Eastbourne
East Lothian	Eastleigh
Eccles	Eccles

The first result is obtained by taking the letters of each name one by one, not bothering if the name consists of more than one word, as in East Ham. This is 'letter by letter' alphabetical arrangement. The second result is obtained by taking the letters of each name one by one again, but, when the name consists of more than one word, going no further than the end of the first word. If there are several names consisting of more than one word, as in the example, then the process is repeated with the second words of the names. This is 'word by word' alphabetical arrangement.

The second point about the arrangement of catalogue sequences in alphabetical order that the reader should note is to do with the way cards are usually filed within a particular author's name. The cards for books the author has written will come first, arranged alphabetically by title. Then will come cards for any books the author has written in conjunction with other authors, next the books he has edited, translated, etc. Finally there will come cards for books other people have written about him.

The third point is that when authors, subjects, and titles have the same name, the order of filing the cards is not strictly alphabetical, but follows the order given in the example below.

a. authors when persons	MANCHESTER, William
b. subjects when persons	MANCHESTER, William
c. authors when places	MANCHESTER UNIVERSITY
d. subjects when places	MANCHESTER UNIVERSITY
e. title	MANCHESTER OF YESTERDAY

There are many other points about alphabetical arrangement, some of them admittedly minor ones, that could be explained. Four only, however, will be mentioned. The first is that headings consisting of abbreviations precede all other words beginning with that letter. e.g.:

B.B.
B.S.A.
BANKS, John

The second is that when titles of books begin with 'A' or 'The', these words are ignored, and the card filed under the next word of the title. For example, the title card for the book *A Reed Shaken by the Wind* would be found under the word 'reed'. The third is that books by authors with names beginning with M', Mc, and Mac are filed in one sequence under 'Mac', e.g.:

> Macaulay
> McDonald
> McIntyre
> MacTaggart

The fourth is that books by authors with double barrelled names like Sheila Kaye-Smith, or names with a prefix like Daphne du Maurier, are usually placed under the first part of the name. The library in its decision is influenced by the Cataloguing Code that it follows. These codes, of which the most important was drawn up by a group of English and American librarians together and is therefore called the Anglo-American Code, list all difficulties that can crop up when a book is being catalogued and indicate the best solutions. With complicated authors' names there is always a reference from the heading that has not been used to the one that has. The term 'references' needs to be explained. If a library places its books by Daphne du Maurier under du Maurier, then there will be placed in the catalogue under Maurier a card reading

> MAURIER, Daphne du
> *see*
> DU MAURIER, Daphne

There are many references like this one in every catalogue, and they are termed 'see references'. There is also another kind of reference card to be found. This is the 'see also reference' type. This second kind will be found, for example, by readers looking in a Dictionary Catalogue for books on all aspects of gardening. At the end of the general gardening books listed under the heading GARDENING, there will be a reference card as shown below.

> GARDENING
> *see also* books on individual branches
> of gardening, e.g. ROSES

The guidance given so far in this chapter will enable readers to find the actual card in the catalogue that they are looking for. The next section of this chapter is concerned with describing the details to be found on catalogue cards.

THE CATALOGUE CARD

The descriptive matter about a book which is found on the catalogue card is known as the catalogue entry. In some libraries catalogue entries are more detailed than in others, and obviously there is a greater need for information in libraries such as large reference libraries, where the reader has to make his choice without seeing the book, than in libraries where all the books are on the public shelves. The card below giving the description of a book is taken from a catalogue entry in the *British National Bibliography*. The service provided by this organization enables libraries to copy the details needed for their catalogues as well as class numbers. They can even buy ready-made catalogue cards.

Books are described in a set way, and in order to fit as much information as possible into the space, certain standard abbreviations, are used. The interpretation of the description is now given, stage by stage, using the example set out in Figure 3:

---

1) 914.21g   **2)** PIPER, David

3) The companion guide to London, by David Piper. Revised ed. **4)** London: Fontana, 10/– 1970. SBN 00 632309 x

5) 520p, 16 plates. illus. maps, plan. 19cm. Pbk. bibl p483–485; index (Companion guides)

6) Previous ed. (B64–22384), London: Collins, 1964.

                              7) (B70–13976)

Key: 1) Class number. 2) Author.   3) Title.   4) Imprint.
        5) Collation.   6) Notes.   7) BNB number.

3. A catalogue card

1. *Class number*

914.21g.

The British National Bibliography, commonly known by its initials, BNB, classifies by the Dewey Decimal Classification, but until 1971 used additional symbols, such as the 'g' at the end of the above number. Libraries also often add symbols of their own to the basic classification number. A symbol placed before the classification, e.g. f914.21, usually means that the book is not shelved with the main sequence of books. An 'f' or a 'q' before the class number indicates that the book is a folio or a quarto respectively, both of which are types of books that because of their size are seldom shelved with the main sequence. If there is any other symbol before the class number, then it will indicate that the book is shelved in reserve, or perhaps in a special collection. There should be a key to such symbols near the catalogue. If there is a symbol after the class number, it will be a means of identifying the book in question from all the other books in the library. As the same class number is given to all books on a particular subject, a library will have several books at each class number. Some libraries prefer to arrange the books within a single class number not alphabetically by author, but by giving each book its own number. Published systems are available to libraries wishing to do this. The result of applying one of them to the book by Piper would give a result like 914.21g P7. As can be seen, a space is left between the classification number and the book number in order to show where the one ends and the other begins.

2. *Author*

PIPER, David

In many catalogues there is one card that gives more information about the book than any other. This is called the Main card or entry, and is placed under the author's name, as this is the most important item in the description of a book. The details given on the card concerning the author will consist of the surname followed by the full Christian names (if known). If the person only acted as editor or compiler, etc., then this will be indicated. If the author uses a pseudonym this will be shown. If the book has more than one author, the main entry card will be placed under the author whose name appears first on the title page of the book. If the book does not have an author, then the main card will be placed under the title of the book, e.g.

A LEGAL bibliography of the British
Commonwealth of Nations

If no author appears on the title page because the book has been published by an organization like the Mathematical Association, or by a government department, or if the author is a paid official of an organization or department, then the main card will be placed under the name of the body responsible for the publication.

MATHEMATICAL ASSOCIATION
The teaching of trigonometry in schools

Government departments, incidentally, are normally entered under the name of the country as in the example below.

GREAT BRITAIN. *Department of Education and Science*
The health of the school child

---

3. *Title*

The companion guide to London, by David Piper. Revised ed.

The title of the book is given in full unless it is very long. The title is always copied from the title page. This title may differ slightly from the title on the outside of the book. At the end of the title is given the edition of the book (if it is not the first). The edition is indicated in an abbreviated form, e.g. 4th ed.

Some catalogue entries, like those in the British National Bibliography, repeat the author's name at the end of the title.

4. *Imprint*

London: Fontana, 10/– 1970. sbn 00 632309 x.

This is the name given to the next section of the description. It consists of the place where the book was published, the name of the publisher, the date of publication, and sometimes the price. If the library does not fully describe its books, only the date of publication may be given. Sometimes two dates are given, one being the date of the contents of the book, the other the date the copy actually was printed, e.g.: 1950 (repr. 1959). The abbreviation 'repr.' is short for reprinted. The details of the book given in the imprint are often important factors in judging the quality of the book. The importance of the date is obvious, as out-of-date books are seldom as useful as more recent ones, but the name of the publisher is also important. Some publishers can be relied upon to produce sound and accurate works, and in certain branches of literature, medical books for instance, some libraries choose their books more by publisher than by author.

At the end of the imprint, British National Bibliography entries add the Standard Book Number (sbn is short for these three words). Standard Book Numbers are explained in detail in the next chapter. Their value is that they enable published works to be individually identified in a shorthand manner.

5. *Collation*

520p, 16 plates. illus. maps, plan. 19cm.
Pbk. bibl p483–485; index (Companion guides)

This part of the description looks like a secret code at first. It is called the collation because it describes the number of pages, the illustrations, and other contents of the book. It does this with the aid of a large number of abbreviations. Some library catalogues omit the collation, or give only a summary of it. The collation first states if the book is in more than one volume, e.g. 3v. It should be noted that v. 3 stands for volume 3, and not for three volumes. The collation next states the number of pages in the book. Often the pages at the front of a book, those containing the list of contents and similar matter, are numbered separately from the rest of the pages. In the collation the number of these is given first before the number of pages in the main sequence. e.g. xii, 308 p. The collation then goes on to consider the illustrations in the book. If the book is illustrated the catalogue may just state 'illus.', but a full description will indicate the kind and sometimes the number of the illustrations. After information on illustrations, the collation of our example states the size of the work (19cm). This is done by giving the height of the book in centimetres to the nearest half-centimetre. It then goes on to indicate that the publication we are considering is a paperback (Pbk.), and that it has both a bibliography (bibl p483–485) and an index. The final item in our collation is the series title (Companion guides). So, if books belong to a publisher's series, this information is given at the end of the collation, within curved brackets.

6. *Notes*

Previous ed. (B64–22384), London: Collins, 1964.

This section of the description is optional. Notes only appear when the cataloguer thinks they will be of use. There are various kinds of notes, some are like the above example, others list the contents of a book, for example, when it contains several plays.

7. *BNB Number*

(B70–13976)

All works entered in the British National Bibliography are given a running number, B70–13976 indicates that this book was the 13,976th to be listed in the bibliography during 1970.

Three final points concerning catalogue cards remain to be considered. The first concerns Annotations. These are summaries of subject matter and sometimes appear on catalogue cards underneath the catalogue entry.

The second point concerns Added Entries. This is the name given to all cards in the catalogue other than the main entry card under the author's name. Added entry cards can sometimes be differentiated from the main card as they contain less information about the book, most of the collation being omitted for example. They can also be differentiated as they contain the added entry heading right at the top of the card, which space is blank on the main card. An added entry that might be found in the name (or author) sequence of a Classified Catalogue for the book under discussion, Piper's *Companion Guide to London,* is shown below.

COMPANION GUIDE TO LONDON
914·21g PIPER, David
The Companion Guide to London

The third point concerns three abbreviations, or rather symbols, that have not yet been considered. They are : [ ], [sic], and .... Square brackets are often found on catalogue cards. They are used whenever the cataloguer wishes to add to the entry words that do not appear on the title page of the book. The sign [sic] indicates some mistake, perhaps in spelling, in the wording on the title page of the book (which must be copied exactly). The sign of the three dots indicates that words appearing on the title page have been omitted from the catalogue card. This is seldom done except where books have very long titles.

The information contained on catalogue cards has been described in detail as it is valuable information, and readers, at least those who use large research libraries, should know the meaning of every item.

The arrangement of other library materials

Throughout this book, the importance of materials other than books is stressed. It is fitting therefore that the arrangement of these materials should now be considered briefly. The arrangement of them is often different from the arrangement of books, as physically they differ in many ways from books. There are fourteen materials to be considered. Those most related to books will be considered first.

NEWSPAPERS AND PERIODICALS

These form an important part of the stock of many libraries, and some libraries stock thousands of them. Libraries usually have special fittings to shelve newspapers, but if a library takes only a few periodicals it may just lay them on tables. If many are taken, there will be separate shelving on which they can be arranged either alphabetically or by subject. The expression 'by subject' means they can be shelved equally well alphabetically by subject, or classified by subject. Near the shelves containing them, there will be an index of them. Many newspapers and periodicals are kept by libraries for only a short period, but if they are kept for any length of time the issues for a year or so are bound together in a volume which is then shelved with the library's books. An entry is made in the library's catalogue for all that are bound.

NEWSPAPER AND PERIODICAL CLIPPINGS

It is usual to arrange these under subject in a box file or in a vertical file. The clippings on each particular subject will be kept together by being placed in a folder. Alternatively they may be pasted chronologically into Clippings' Books and an index compiled to the books.

PAMPHLETS

It is not easy to decide where books end and pamphlets begin, though librarians sometimes consider any work of less than fifty pages a pamphlet. The following comparisons may be made. Books have stiff covers, pamphlets paper covers; books are bound, pamphlets are thin enough to be stapled. Pamphlets may be treated like books, classified like them, catalogued like them, and shelved like them. Often, however, they are placed in a box or vertical file with the library's clippings. When pamphlets are not entered in the catalogue, some other index will be made of them. Two special types of pamphlets need mention at this point. The first, holiday guides, because these will be found arranged alphabetically under resort; and the second, patent specifications, as these will be found arranged by the running number of the specification.

MANUSCRIPTS

Many libraries contain manuscripts and a few are officially approved as places where manuscripts and other archive material can be deposited. Manuscripts will always be available to readers, but they will usually be kept in a strongroom. They will be catalogued, but not always classified. A similar class of material to manuscripts is theses, and all university libraries value their collections of these unpublished works of research.

MAPS

Because of their size maps are shelved flat in large shallow drawers or in vertical files. They may also be shelved rolled up in frames that look like an oversize visible index or, if they form part of a map series, bound with the series to form a large book. Maps are usually arranged by continent and country, and not by subject. A list, possibly in the form of a visible index, will indicate what is available.

SHEET MUSIC

Sheets will be kept in visible or box files, and arranged in the same way as the books of music. There will be catalogue entries for it.

ILLUSTRATIONS

Collections of loose illustrations will usually be kept in box or vertical files. The arrangement will be by subject. An index may not be provided.

MICROTEXTS

These are books, or other printed documents, which have been photographed and reproduced very much reduced in size. The reproduction will be on film of some sort or on card. In either case a machine will be needed to enlarge the microtext before it can be read. Microtexts are becoming more and more widely used, partly because they make it possible to reproduce, at a reasonable cost, a few copies of out-of-print material, but mainly because they take up so little space. This is an important advantage, as research libraries seldom throw anything away. A microtext containing the issues of a daily newspaper for a whole year can be fitted into a box no larger than an average sized book, and modern developments will soon enable this type of reduction to seem but a slight one.

Microtexts are made in several forms, of which three may be distinguished: microfilms, sheet microfilms, and microcards. Microfilms, which are wound on spools like any other film, are kept in boxes about the size of a small book. Sheet microfilm, as the name suggests, will be best preserved in envelopes, kept flat by being placed in a vertical file. Both these forms of microtexts will have details of their contents on the outsides of the containers. They will usually be given entries in the main catalogue. The containers may be arranged by the classification scheme, or by an accession number. An accession number is a running number given to an item of library stock when it is acquired. Microcards are rather different in that they are the size of catalogue cards and contain their own catalogue entry at the top of them. They may therefore simply be placed in catalogue card drawers in any required order.

GRAMOPHONE RECORDS

These are arranged by composer or classified in some way. If the readers have to choose their records without being able to handle them, they may also be arranged by accession number. They will be shelved as in gramophone shops. The catalogue of them will probably be in the form of a visible index, and when readers are not allowed to browse amongst the records, it will incorporate some method of indicating whether records are available for borrowing.

TAPE RECORDINGS AND VIDEOTAPES

The former reproduce sounds, the latter vision as well. Recordings now usually come in cassette form and are therefore easily handled. If they are of music, they will be arranged in their boxes, either under composer or subject. An index similar to the one for gramophone records will probably be available.

FILMS

Films will be kept in tins or boxes alphabetically under title. There will be an index of them available, possibly similar to the one for gramophone records.

Serving adults: Devizes Regional Branch Library, showing telex machine

2. Serving children: 'And then the sun came out', story time for the under fives at a Wandsworth Public Library

A home from home: Lincoln Teenage Library, showing records and paperbacks

Books for loan: Mobile Library at Littlebeck, Yorkshire North Riding

5. Staff assistance: Information Centre, Bishop Street, Leicester City Libraries
6. Facilities for study: Commercial Library at Holborn Central Library

7. Using microtexts: City
of Liverpool Public Library

8. Photocopying facilities:
Central Library, Lincoln

9. Records and pictures for loan: Kentish Town Branch, Camden Public Libraries

10. Aid to handicapped readers: Hackney's Hospital Library Service

hester : History
ue town that I knew in my youth. 2. Moss Side. Ernest Irlam. 3.
Northender. Albert E. Bracegirdle. 4. Openshaw. E. Cooke. Manches-
er R., 11 (Autumn/Winter, 1968) p.193-210
hester : History
ated Headings :
    Banks, Isabella
hester : Port
't invests in the future. Times. (4 Jun 69) p.vii
erston
ated Headings :
    Gardens and Gardening : Scotland : Manderston
evilie, Bernard
ibliographical note on Bernard Mandeville's *Free Thoughts*. Irwin
'rimer. Notes and Queries, 16 (May 69) p.187-8
Made Disasters. See Disasters, Man-Made
Made Fibre Industry
e wool price and the production of synthetics. A.C. Rayner.
orkshire Bulletin, 21 (May 69) p.31-8, il. refs.
Made Fibre Industry
ated Headings :
    Carbon Fibre Industry
Made Fibre Industry : Great Britain
ated Headings :
    Crimplene Fibre Industry : Great Britain
ng, Olivia
o is Olivia Manning? Ruth Inglis. Observer. (6 Apr 69) colour suppt.
.24-7, il.
ial Rolls : Man, Isle of
early manorial roll. Michael Crellin. Manx Museum J., 7 (1969)
.98-9
ower
knowledge society. Peter F. Drucker. New Society. (24 Apr 69)
.629-31
ower
ated Headings :
    International Labour Organization
    Unemployment
ower : Great Britain
and disequilibrium in the labour market and wage rate inflation in the
nited Kingdom. 1. A.P. Thirlwall. Yorkshire Bulletin, 21 (May 69)
.66-76, il. refs.
ower Mobility
ase study in labour mobility. R.M. Jones. Manchester School of
conomic and Social Studies, 37 (Jun 69) p.169-74. refs.
cripts, English
ated Headings :
    Doyle, Sir Arthur Conan
    Royal Commission on Historical Manuscripts
    Somerset Record Office
cripts, Music. See Music : Manuscripts
Languages
ated Headings :
    Bird Names
'se-Tung
's attributes. Edgar Snow. Listener. (29 May 69) p.757
England : London
atlas of London : problems of compilation. Dorothy Castle and
ine Fielding. East London Papers, 11 (Winter 68) p.85-93. il.
Great Britain
y maps as historical evidence for coastal change. G. De Boer and
.P. Carr. Geographical J., 135 (Mar 69) p.17-39. refs.
Great Britain
ated Headings :
    Ordnance Survey
History
orative early maps. Brian J. Page. Antique Collector, 40 (Apr-May
9) p.63-6, il.
New Zealand
e New Zealand maps and statistical sources. J.A. Dawson.
eography, 54 (Apr 69) p.198-203
Scotland
ated Headings :
    Pont, Timothy
se, Herbert
cuse and revolution, Alasdair Clayre. Observer. (18 May 69) p.38+.
.
ne Aggression
power politics. Charles Douglas-Home. Times. (25 Apr 69) p.10
Deutsche. See Deutschemark
ge
iage. Anthony Quinton. Listener. 81 (10 Apr 69) p.483-4
arried couples. Jenny Maitland-Jones. Times. (11 Jun 69) p.13
married couples grow alike. Martin Herbert. New Society.
Apr 69) p.518-21

Marriage—cont.
Related Headings :
    Divorce
    Weddings
Marriage : Great Britain : Law
The validation of void marriages. D. Tolstoy. Modern Law R., 31
(Nov 68) p.656-61
Marriage : India
Battle for a matchmaker. Joseph Minogue. Guardian, (2 Apr 69) p.7
Marriage : New Zealand : Law
That monstrous animal a husband and wife : notes on recent
matrimonial legislation. Donald Dugdale. Landfall, No.89 (Mar 69)
p.61-9. refs.
Marriage Guidance
Marriages on probation. Geoffrey Parkinson. New Society. (22 May 69)
p.795-6
Married Women. See Women, Married
Martinelli, Giovanni
Giovanni Martinelli, 1885-1969. Dame Eva Turner, Francis Robinson, and
Sir John Barbirolli. Opera, 20 (Apr 69) p.290-3, port.
Marvell, Andrew
Andrew Marvell : *Upon the Hill and Grove at Bill-Borow and Musicks
Empire*. A.J.N. Wilson. John Rylands Library Bulletin, 51
(Spring 69) p.453-82. refs.
Marvin, Blanche
To start with the groundlings. Auriol Stevens. Guardian, (7 Apr 69) p.7
Marx, Karl
The political economy of alienation : Karl Marx and Adam Smith. E.G.
West. Oxford Economic Papers, 21 (Mar 69) p.1-23. refs.
Portrait of a bibliophile : Karl Marx and Friedrich Engels. Book
Collector, 18 (Summer 69) p.189-99. il. refs.
Teilhard, China and neo-Marxism. Ernan McMullin. Month, 41 (May 69)
p.274-85, refs.
Mary, Queen of Scots
Daughter of debate. [*Mary Queen of Scots*, by Antonia Fraser].
A.S. Byatt. New Statesman, (16 May 69) p.693-4
Exquisite princess. [*Mary Queen of Scots*, by Antonia Fraser].
V.G. Kiernan. Listener, 81 (1 May 69) p.616-17
Mary, Mary, quite contrary. Roy Strong. Spectator, (16 May 69) p.648-9.
port.
Marylebone Cricket Club
How the Gentlemen were caught out. Ivan Yates. Observer. (13 Apr 69)
p.10
Mass Demonstrations
Related Headings :
    Student Demonstrations
Mass Demonstrations : Northern Ireland
Bottle bombs in Derry battle. Mary Holland. Observer. (20 Apr 69) p.1
Mass Media (Culture)
Dissent, disobedience and the mass media. 2. Karl Miller. Listener, 81
(1 May 69) p.602-3
Massachusetts
Related Headings :
    Concord
Massingberd, Frances Charles
F.C. Massingberd : historian in a Lincolnshire parish. W.J. Baker.
Lincolnshire History and Archaeology, 3 (1968) p.3-10. refs.
Matchan, Leonard
The man on the end of the phone. Geoffrey Nicholson. Nova,
(May/Jun 69) p.100+. il.
Materialism. (Philosophy)
Faith and materialism. Margaret Laws-Smith. Humanist, 84 (May 69)
p.149-51
Materialism (Philosophy)
Related Headings :
    Christianity and Materialism
Mathematics : History
Related Headings :
    Babbage, Charles
Matrimonial Property : Law
Spouse traps. R.A. Cline. Spectator. (9 May 69) p.613-14
Maud Report. See Local Government : Great Britain : Reform
Mauritius
Mauritius—a survey : Jewel of the Indian Ocean. Patrick Keatley ;
Colourful diversity of culture ; Planning for the future ; Political
brinkmanship ; Land of rainbows and blue lagoons ; The flamboyant
leaders. Guardian, (27 May 69) p.9-12, il.
Mauritius
Related Headings :
    Tourism : Mauritius
Mauritius : Economics
Planning for the future. Guardian, (27 May 69) p.10
Mauritius : Politics and Government
The flamboyant leaders. Guardian, (27 May 69) p.12
Political brinkmanship. Guardian, (27 May 69) p.10

An index to periodical articles (from: *British Humanities Index 2*, April–June,
9)

How to use statistics   **2282**

by P. G. MOORE

Management Today, January 1970,
pp. 53-5. (UK)

Traditionally, managers have accepted accounting data as being accurate enough to be used for making precise decisions, but have distrusted statistical data often considering them almost valueless for decision-making purposes. In the past few years, however, faith in accounting data has been shaken by, for example, the GEC/AEI struggle and the Leasco/Pergamon affair. Both these examples emphasise the problem of the meaning that can be given to financial figures. The same commodities can be given different values on different balance sheets but not many managers appreciate these discrepancies.

How should managers tackle the problem? In the first place they should examine financial data from three angles (a) are there any causes of bias in the methods? (b) is the sampling procedure satisfactory to provide the desired accuracy? and (c) what elements in the data are subjective assessments and how important are they to the overall data?

Once recognition of the need for serious consideration of the accuracy of data has been established, how can they be examined in an accounting framework? The thinking which should go before this procedure is illustrated with case examples.

(Photocopy 4s. 6d)

Group capacity assessment   **2283**

by B. C. G. PEARCE

O & M Bulletin, February 1970,
pp. 39-49. (UK)

An office work measurement technique known as Group Capacity Assessment (GCA) has recently been employed by the Ministry of Defence in a branch of the department covering some 90 clerical staff, mainly engaged in the validation of claims from contractors and the resultant bill paying function. The theory behind GCA is that the clerical functions of a group can be split into separate portions of work and related to units of output. Conventional work measurement

techniques can be used to establish 'shoul take' times for average trained clerical worker at standard performance. These includ time study and various forms of work samp ling, particularly fixed interval sampling.

However, the standards used are for grou control purposes and not for the assessmen of individuals. The input/output of work i monitored as necessary to provide a basi for the assessment of effectiveness of th group concerned. It is easier to install offic work measurement techniques in areas whe the work is routine and repetitive, but th experience described shows that it can b applied even where the work is varied an includes a considerative element. The applica tion of GCA is unlikely to be rewarding whe applied to isolated pockets of fewer tha five clerical staff.

The method of operating the system described. Consultants were employed t train existing staff of the department in th appropriate techniques. This lasted thre weeks. Five analysts were required for eac 100 staff to be measured. The method an the results are presented and discussed charts illustrate the different stages of th work. The objective of GCA is that it provide management with a *continuing* form control based on measured output. Once it installed, an average of five minutes a da per clerical staff is considered sufficie to maintain it. In the branch in question th scheme has worked well, and has give satisfaction to management and staff alike.

(Photocopy 13s. 6

What communication means   **228**

by PETER DRUCKER

Management Today, March 1970,
pp. 91-3, 150-1. (UK)

Communication in industry has been th subject of an ever-increasing amount research and publications, but it is unde stood by hardly any of the people involve Despite all the work that has been don industrial communications appear to be le effective now than at any other time.

This is partly because of the informatio explosion and partly because the failure systems adopted hitherto has given rise to

FILM STRIPS

These will also be kept in their containers, but may be arranged by subject, rather than alphabetically by title. An index, similar to the one to films, will be available.

SLIDES

Slides are likely to deal with local history, and will be arranged under subject. They will be kept in drawers and an index of them will be available to readers.

LEARNING KITS

These are rather different from all the other library materials dealt with in this section, and so have been left to the end. A learning kit will consist of printed information, probably in book or pamphlet form, supported by audio-visual materials, such as gramophone records. The value of such kits for learning languages, for example, is obvious, and libraries will increasingly stock them. However, because they consist of more than one type of library material, they can cause problems of arrangement, and may therefore not be on open-access.

Programmed learning, which is a method of step-by-step learning, usually on a teach-yourself basis, may make use of a learning kit, though this type of learning commonly uses specially designed learning machines. The library of the future will probably lend out learning machines as well as supplying the programmes to put in them.

Non-book materials, it can now be seen, are not always classified and catalogued like the library's bookstock. This is partly because they do not lend themselves to conventional classification and cataloguing due to their physical form, but also because library users do not always want the same information about non-book materials as they do about books. In particular they will often be more interested in a subject approach than an author one. In recent years, therefore, considerable attention has been paid to ways of analysing the subject content of library materials in greater depth than is possible using ordinary

3

classification and cataloguing techniques. Pamphlet material, such as technical reports, has been especially singled out for treatment. As such pamphlet material is most intensively used in special libraries, it is libraries of this type that have developed the new methods of subject analysis most thoroughly.

There are several alternative methods of subject analysis, but all allow a reader to find precisely what is available on a highly specialized topic, and nearly all use special equipment from punched cards to computers.

Systems of arranging and indexing library materials by these methods, are usually known as information retrieval systems. A tremendous amount of research is being carried out on information retrieval, and many complicated systems are already available, but they are not likely to be met with in the average library.

BOOKS FOR FURTHER STUDY

Anglo-American Cataloguing Rules: British text. Library Association, 1967.
COLLISON, R. L. *Commercial and Industrial Storage.* Benn, 1969. In spite of its title deals well with the arrangement of non-book materials.
Dewey Decimal Classification. 18th ed. New York, Forest Press, 1971. Like the first title listed here, for examining and reference rather than for reading.
NEEDHAM, C. D. *Organizing Knowledge in Libraries.* 2nd ed. Deutsch, 1971.
Covers both classification and cataloguing.

Chapter 4
What every reader should know

About reading

Everybody who studies this book undoubtedly knows how to read. But a good reader is more than somebody who knows how to read. He also knows about all the forms that reading takes, and he is a master of the various skills that make for efficient reading. An outline of types of reading and of the reading skills appropriate to those types will now be given. Perhaps, after studying this section, you will find you have time to read more things than you could before, and also obtain more enjoyment and satisfaction from your reading.

Whether you read with efficiency and enjoyment does not depend altogether on yourself. The author and the publisher can both hinder your reading. The author can make an easy subject difficult to understand by bad writing. The publisher can make a book difficult to follow by designing it poorly.

Efficient reading is done with the brain not the eyes. Indeed, the eyes are capable of reading whole books in no time at all. What limits reading speed is the ability of the mind to translate the letters the eyes see into meaningful thoughts and information. True, the brain can be trained to accept reading speeds far higher than those used by the average reader, and a high reading speed is one of the marks of the master reader. But, if there is a particular quality that sets the efficient reader apart from the inefficient one, it is that of flexibility. An efficient reader is one who uses a variety of reading speeds and techniques. Above all, he decides exactly his reason for reading the book or article in front of him, and suits his reading style to this.

There are many reasons why people read. They read to pass examinations, to understand instructions, to see if they have read a book previously, to memorize a poem, to put themselves to sleep. And, of course, different people may read the same work for different reasons (and, indeed, an individual may read it for one reason on one occasion and for another reason on another). This means that in everyday life there is tremendous scope for flexibility in reading. Reasons for reading are now grouped and discussed under four headings: Recreational reading, Reading for specific facts, Reading to comprehend, and Critical reading. These are the four main types of reading and they have been arranged here in ascending order of difficulty. They have been so arranged to save repetition, for many of the skills used in the simpler types of reading are also relevant to the more difficult types.

RECREATIONAL READING

Recreational reading is reading for relaxation, reading that we choose to do rather than that we have to do. It is reading done for pleasure, though we should find pleasure too in other kinds of reading. With recreational reading, unlike with the other types we will discuss, there are few rules to obey, since enjoyment and not efficiency predominates. Fiction is the most popular type of recreational reading, and, of course, there is plenty of fiction available in magazines as well as in books. However, some people prefer to relax with biographical, historical, and travel stories, rather than with fiction. Most recreational reading material is written in an easy style that enables a fairly fast reading pace to be maintained. And, as the subject matter is usually straightforward, the mind and the memory can work without conscious effort. Sometimes, though, a word will be met with that is unknown to you. Don't stop reading immediately and rush to look it up in a dictionary. Continue to the end of the paragraph, and you will often find that you are able to understand the meaning of the word from the context in which it is placed. However, if when you have reached the end of the paragraph you still have no idea of its meaning, look it up in your dictionary. Good readers have good vocabularies.

Should a bookmark be used? Yes, as it means you can begin reading exactly where you left off, without having to spend time finding your place. And, if you use a plain piece of paper (or thin card), you can make comments on it as you read. You won't usually want to make many during recreational reading, but you might write on your bookmark the meaning of those words you had to look up in a dictionary. Doing this will help fix the words' meanings in your mind and, as you keep seeing these definitions whenever you open your book, your memory will be further reinforced by the time you have completed reading it.

READING FOR SPECIFIC FACTS

Reading for specific facts is reading to locate a certain fact or facts in a piece of writing – looking up telephone numbers or addresses, checking the spelling of a word you are using in a letter. It is an unusual form of reading as instead of having to work systematically through pages and paragraphs, you just look for particular words or figures. Unless you know exactly where in a publication the desired facts are to be found, the technique of scanning must be used. Scanning is running the eyes quickly over the lines of print until required information is located. The eyes then begin reading normally. Reading for specific facts, unlike the other types of reading here considered, requires, therefore, little use of one's understanding. There is no plot or sequence of author's thoughts to be followed, just certain facts to be found.

When reading for specific facts, pencil and paper come in handy, as you can then jot down the fact when you have found it. After you have jotted it down, check that you have copied it correctly. If the fact you require is difficult to locate because of the way it is presented, for example in a mass of small print, use your pencil (or your finger) to lead your eye down the page to it. Often reading for specific facts involves the use of quick-reference books such as dictionaries and directories. You will locate the fact you want more rapidly if you pay attention to the way the book is arranged, and what guidance it offers to those who use it. The value of contents lists and indexes cannot be overemphasized.

READING TO COMPREHEND

Recreational reading involved following a theme or plot, reading for specific facts involved picking out items of information.

Reading to comprehend necessitates doing both these things at the same time, and can take many forms, for example reading a newspaper in order to find out and understand what is happening in the world today, reading about how to knit a sweater or mend a fuse, reading textbooks in order to succeed in one's studies. It is possible to read to comprehend ideas and attitudes as well as, or instead of, facts. Reading to comprehend gives us considerable scope to use our brains. It also gives considerable scope for us to make full use of a number of efficient reading techniques. Examining these in the order they will be used leads us to consider first previewing. Previewing is looking at what we are about to read before we read it, or looking at reading material to decide if it is worth reading. Previewing can be done with recreational reading, but it belongs more to reading to comprehend. There are three sorts of previewing, as we shall now see.

The first sort is done most quickly and is casual browsing. This sort of previewing consists of glancing in a perfunctory way at reading material in order to see if it is worth spending further time on. It is done by us when we are in a library trying to find a title of interest on the shelves, when we open a newspaper and look at the headlines, when we thumb through a magazine. If we find a book that seems worth reading on the library shelves, then we stop browsing and take the book home (or to a library table) for a further examination. If we find a headline to a news item or magazine article that holds our attention, we likewise cease browsing and with a newspaper item proceed to read it straight through. However, with a magazine article, as with a book, we may still not be sure whether it is worth reading. We therefore take a further look at it.

The result is a purposeful type of browsing, one which consists of looking at chapter and section headings, examining any 'blurb' or summary, and really making sure that the book or article contains something that is of interest to us. This second kind of previewing is not sufficient to give us much knowledge as to what the material is about, but it is sufficient to enable us to make up our minds whether to read it.

The third and final kind of previewing to be considered is skimming. Skimming is carried out for a purpose different from that of the other two forms of previewing, and it is used only with Reading to comprehend and Critical reading. Its purpose in fact is to enable the mind to assess how the author has organized his material and at the same time see the outline or skeleton of the publication. When the real reading starts, the mind, as a result of this skim, already has its bearings and so works more effectively.

Skimming should be carried out for an article by reading the title (and sub-titles if any), the opening paragraph, subsequent headings, and the closing paragraph. If there are few headings, and the article is only short, read the opening sentence of every paragraph. The opening sentence often contains the gist of the paragraph. With a book, skimming should consist of reading the title (and sub-titles if any), the contents page, the author's introduction, and then sampling the text, especially the opening and closing pages.

With Reading to comprehend and Critical reading, follow the previewing by pausing for a moment and asking yourself questions like: Why am I doing this reading? What does it seem the author has to offer? How much do I already know about the topic? The reason for using the technique of questioning is that it makes the mind more aware of what it needs to find and do during the reading you are about to begin.

During the reading of the book or article continue to ask questions. Pause from time to time to remind yourself of what you have learnt and ask questions such as: Have I understood all that I have read? If you come across paragraphs that obviously deal with information or ideas that you know already, increase your reading pace to a scanning rate and continue to scan until you reach material that contains something new to you. If, from your preview, you find that whole sections of the work are irrelevant to your needs, do not hesitate to skip them altogether.

When reading to comprehend, have a pencil handy and mark any places you want to refer to again with a mark in the margin. (If the book you are reading is not your own, use your bookmark to note the page numbers that you want, rather than mark the pages themselves.) Incidentally, if you hold your pencil in your hand whilst you read, you may find that not only is it convenient for making marginal marks (and perhaps comments), but that it also helps you concentrate. Critical reading, as we shall see, demands most thought and concentration, but reading to comprehend undoubtedly calls for an active mind, and, to some extent, a critical mind. It calls for a mind that thinks, 'That's a good point', or 'That doesn't make sense', as the reading takes place.

At the end of the book or article, don't put the publication down and virtually forget it. Instead, think about what you have read, and in particular ask yourself whether you have found out what you wanted, and if you have grasped all that the author has had to say. Doing this is known as reviewing what you have read. As a result of your review you may feel that you need to re-read parts of what you have read. You may also decide to examine those places where you have made marks in the margin.

Reading to comprehend sometimes involves the memorizing of facts or even passages. Then further re-reading will obviously be necessary. In addition, consider saying the words you need to memorize out loud as you read. Your memory thereby hears as well as sees what it has to remember, and this double impression aids the process of memorizing.

CRITICAL READING

Critical reading is the most advanced type of reading and consists of two processes, understanding and appreciating. Critical reading necessitates the techniques discussed under Reading to comprehend, but also necessitates being able to analyse and evaluate an author's facts and ideas. Critical reading is done, to give some examples, by students of literature, by teachers marking students' work, and by book reviewers. It is a kind of reading that must be done in two stages, as the understanding process must precede the appreciation one. After all, you can only relate what you have read to your own ideas and experience, and see the strengths and weaknesses of the writing, when you have comprehended it. Typical questions to be asked at the appreciation stage are: What is the author's position, attitudes and bias? What are my attitudes compared with his? Has the reading affected my attitudes? Does the author present his facts and ideas adequately, or does he make mistakes, omissions, and write badly?

Critical reading may involve a re-reading after such questions have been asked and thought about. This re-reading enables you to make a double-check on whether any important points have been missed, and on whether your appreciation is valid and fair.

Having looked at the various forms that reading takes, and noted that each calls for a different approach by the reader, it remains to look at one more thing. It is that good readers not only choose the right approach to whatever they are reading, they steer clear of bad reading habits. Two common reading faults are word-by-word reading and regression. In addition, many readers pay too little attention to the physical factors that affect their reading, such as their surroundings.

Word-by-word reading is letting the eyes stop and look at each word being read. It is a bad habit because words are not important in themselves, it is units of meaning that are important. These normally consist of a group of words, perhaps a phrase. If we try to read every word as a word, our reading will be slow, and we will be in danger of not seeing the wood for the trees. Word-by-word readers tend to say each word to themselves as they read; you can sometimes see their lips moving. Looking for and reading units of meaning rather than individual words will reduce this tendency to vocalization.

Regression is going backwards and re-reading the line or sentence just read. The usual reason for regression is lack of understanding of what has been read. Regression is natural, especially when reading about unfamiliar and difficult topics, but it must be kept to a minimum. If it is not, our reading becomes slow and gives us less satisfaction. To keep regression at a minimum, use the same technique as that used when you meet a word whose meaning you did not know: read on and see if the context makes things clear.

The effect of physical surroundings on the efficiency of our reading should be obvious. Reading by candlelight, for example, is not to be recommended. To read efficiently you need reasonable light. You also need warmth and comparative quiet. It is true that there are a few people who can read oblivious to everything around them, but it is better for most of us to find a place (especially for serious reading) where we can concentrate easily.

If you have a great deal of reading to get through, don't overdo it. Give the eyes and the brain regular short breaks. What reading time you lose having these breaks will be more than made up by fatigue being reduced.

Finally, what was stated at the start of this section should be repeated. The mark of an efficient reader is flexibility in reading skills and speeds. And so lack of such flexibility is as much a reading fault as those discussed above. Therefore, whenever you are about to read, remember to decide your purpose in reading at the start, and then you can draw up a reading plan enabling you to achieve that purpose effectively.

About books

THE PARTS OF A BOOK

The following brief examination of the parts of a book is made from a reader's point of view. The printed parts of a book are of most interest to readers, but, before considering them, let us take a quick look at the physical make-up of a book.

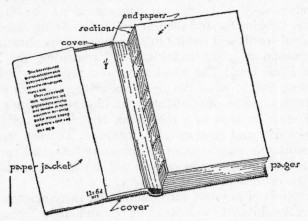

4. The physical components of a book

The physical make-up

If a book, preferably an unwanted one, is taken to pieces, three distinct parts are revealed. The first part, which is only folded round the cover of the book, is the paper book jacket.

This jacket, which nearly all books are now given, serves not only to keep the book clean, but acts as a powerful form of publicity for the book. Paperback books make up for their lack of book jacket by sporting brightly-illustrated covers. The second part is the cover itself. This part usually consists of a stiff paper board covered with cloth and attached to the pages of the book by a strip of muslin and by the endpapers. The endpapers, which are at each end of the book, have half their width pasted down to the cover of the book and the other half attached to the pages of the book. A good pull will soon detach the cover from the pages of the book; these form the third part. If the backs of the pages, now revealed by the removal of the cover, are examined, it will be found that they are folded together into groups. It will also be seen that the groups of pages are attached to each other, and to the endpapers, by twine. Pull at this twine, and the groups of pages, known to printers as sections, will come loose. The reason for the pages being in groups is that the presses that print the book hold large sheets of paper and print on each several pages of the book. Afterwards the sheets are folded down to the page size of the book. The resulting groups of pages have their backs stitched together, and their other three sides trimmed. Most readers will have come across at some time books that have been inadequately trimmed (or not trimmed at all) and will have had to cut the pages laboriously apart so as to read the book. The terms folio, quarto, and octavo (there are others but these are the three best known terms) are usually thought of as referring to the page size of a book; a folio is a very large book, a quarto a rather large book, and an octavo a normal sized book. The terms are often used in this sense, but originally they referred to the number of times the original sheet of paper had had to be folded in order to form the pages of the book. If it had been folded only once, the book was a folio, if twice, a quarto, if three times, an octavo.

A few books, like telephone directories, are not stitched along their backs after folding, but have all their four sides trimmed. The back edge of all the pages is then coated with a strong adhesive. This method of binding means, of course, that the book has no sections; it also means that single pages can become loose.

If a book is illustrated, the illustrations are sometimes printed on different paper from the rest of the book. When this is done, the illustrations may not be stitched in with the book, but attached only by paste to the other pages.

The parts that are printed

It is customary to divide the printed matter in a book into three sections: Preliminaries, Text-matter and Subsidiaries. These three items will now be explained and the contents of the sections they head considered.

Preliminaries This is the general term given to the items that appear before the first chapter of the book. The preliminary pages are printed after the rest of the book, and are therefore numbered separately or not at all. The items generally appear in the following order, though not all of them will be contained in all books.

(i) *half-title*. When the endpaper at the front of the book is turned over, the first page of the book proper is revealed. Unless there are some blank pages at the front of the book, this page will be the half-title page, and will give the principal words of the title of the book.

(ii) *announcement*. When the half-title is turned over, the second and third pages of the book will be revealed. On the second page a list of other books the author has written, or some such announcement may be printed.

(iii) *frontispiece*. If a book contains a frontispiece, the third page of the book will be the back of the frontispiece and blank. The frontispiece itself always faces the title page.

(iv) *title page*. The title page is important, as it gives the author and full title of the book, along with certain other information such as the date of publication. For this reason it is always printed where it can be seen best, on a right hand page.

(v) *statement of editions*. The title page may give the name and address of the publisher of the book. If it does not, these will often be given on the back of the title page. The name and address of the printer of the book may also be found. The standard information to be found on the back of the title page is, however, the statement of editions. It will be on the following lines:

First published	1935
Second impression	1937
Third impression	1940
Second edition	1945
Second edition reprinted	1957

The first edition of a book is the total number of copies printed, at any time, from the type set up by the printer. All the copies may not be printed at the same time; for example the publisher of the book may find that the book is selling well and so ask the printer to print some additional copies. This second printing from the original type is known as the second impression of the first edition. After a gap of a number of years, the publisher may decide that there is a demand for more copies of the book, though in the meantime he has told the printer to dispose of the type. The publisher has then to decide whether to publish a reprint or a new edition of the book. A reprint is an exact copy of the original book, printed however from new type. A new edition also means that type has to be set up, but in it the subject matter of the original book is brought up to date, or altered in some other way. This means, of course, that it is the date of the last edition of a book that reveals how up to date are the contents of the book. I have used the terms edition, impression, and reprint as librarians use them. In fact, new impressions are sometimes called new editions or reprints by publishers.

The back of the title page will probably also contain a statement on the following lines:

© Copyright John Smith 1960

Such a statement enables the holder of the copyright of a book to claim international copyright protection under the UNESCO agreement of 1952. It serves another purpose too. It enables readers to ascertain the age of a book's contents when the date of edition is not clear.

(vi) *Standard book number.* A scheme of numbering book titles came in during 1968, and virtually all British books now have what is called a Standard Book Number. Usually found on the back of the title page, it may also be given on the rear cover of the book. The scheme was introduced to enable efficient use to be made of computers in the book world, and generally to reduce administrative costs. The book number has three parts: publisher's number, title number, and check digit, in that order, and a gap is left between each part e.g. 08 006688 7. The number is normally prefaced by the initials SBN (short for Standard Book Number). The check digit at the end is to help stop computer errors. A plan is afoot to make Standard Book Numbers international, and some books already contain an International number. These numbers are prefaced by the initials ISBN (International Standard Book Number) and include an extra digit at the front to indicate country group e.g. ISBN 1 08 006688 7. Standard Book Numbers are already given in many bibliographies and publishers' catalogues, and books will be increasingly referred to in this shorthand way.

(vii) *dedication*. On the next page there may be the customary dedication by the author of the book. It will usually be quite simple in form, for example:

To my wife

(viii) *preface, foreword or introduction*. These three terms are used interchangeably at the head of any introductory remarks made either by the author or by a person of note commending the author and his book. It is most usual, however, for the terms preface and introduction to denote matter written by the author, and the term foreword matter written by a person of distinction.

(ix) *acknowledgements*. Help given in the preparation of the book is acknowledged by the author at this point in the Preliminaries. On occasions the acknowledgements are included in the author's introduction, or are given at the back of the book.

(x) *corrections*. The term errata may be used instead. The corrections are sometimes printed on a small piece of paper that does not form part of the original book at all but which is inserted into the Preliminaries. As the Preliminaries are printed after the text-matter of the book, the corrections may alternatively form a page of them proper.

(xi) *list of contents*. This term is self-explanatory; to aid potential readers of the book, the contents of each chapter may briefly be indicated.

(xii) *list of illustrations*. The illustrations having been listed in the same way as the contents, with the appropriate page number alongside each, the Preliminaries come to an end.

Text-matter. The text-matter forms the main part of the book. The title of the book should be given at the head of every alternate page of the text-matter, and the title of the chapter, or section, along the top of every other page.

Subsidiaries. Most books have the majority of the items discussed in the section on the Preliminaries but few books have many Subsidiaries, that is items after the main text-matter. The order of the Subsidiaries is not as fixed as the order of the Preliminaries but many serious non-fiction books will have most of the following items roughly in the order they are given.

(i) *appendices*. These give, in full, documents, such as Acts of Parliament, referred to in the text-matter. They may also be used by the author to enable the detailed story of some event mentioned in the text to be told.

(ii) *notes*. Notes are somewhat similar to appendices, but they are much shorter. Indeed, the majority of books, instead of relegating notes to the Subsidiaries, place them at the bottom or side of each page of the text. Mixed up with the notes will be bibliographic references, which are the details of books the author wishes to mention in connection with his subject. Both notes and references will be linked to the appropriate places in the text by symbols. The subject of bibliographic references is dealt with in detail in Chapter 6.

(iii) *supplement*. This is made up of matter that the author would have placed in the text-matter had he known about it at the time of writing; a supplement is often to be found in a book that has gone through several impressions, the author in the later impressions bringing his book up to date in this way.

(iv) *bibliography*. A bibliography has already been defined as a list of books. The bibliography to a book lists the other books, and possibly periodical articles, on the subject of the book itself, from which the reader can find out further information. The bibliography, which may go under another name, such as 'Books for further reading', is sometimes split up and placed at the end of each chapter. The bibliography may contain a complete or a select list of the books on the subject in question.

(v) *glossary*. This defines technical terms used in the text. For example, a book on printing will often include a glossary of printing terms.

(vi) *indexes*. The word has been given in the plural as some books have more than one index, perhaps one to the subjects mentioned in the book, another to the people mentioned. On the other hand, it is to be regretted that a number of books which ought to have indexes are published without any at all. Indexes are of vital importance to the finding of information in a book, as they analyse the contents of the book in far more detail than can the book's list of contents. Indeed, the objects of the two are complementary. Indexes show the exact places where topics are mentioned throughout the book, whilst contents pages reveal the general theme of the book, and how that theme is developed.

(vii) *colophon*. This was originally the name given to an illustration that acted as the trade mark of the printer of the book. Today, it refers to the details about printing sometimes to be found right at the end of books. It also describes the symbol used by publishers to distinguish their own imprint.

(viii) *advertisements*. There are sometimes spare pages at the back of a book. These may be left blank, but on the other hand the publisher may fill them with details of other books he has produced.

TYPES OF BOOKS

It is difficult to split books into types as one of the qualities that characterizes books is their individuality. However, looking at books from the reader's point of view, certain rough divisions can be made. The main split is obvious, it is into fiction and non-fiction. The divisions of these two main categories are not so obvious, but the following may be considered acceptable.

Fiction

A fiction book is really one in which the author uses his imagination rather than facts. However, the word fiction generally refers only to novels; poems, plays and other such imaginative works being considered as belonging to the literature branch of non-fiction. The word fiction is used in this book in this more restricted sense. Three types of fiction can be distinguished: classical fiction, standard fiction, and light fiction.

Classical fiction is the type that has survived the trials of time. The authors of it are mainly dead, but readers will not forget their work. The names of authors of classical fiction appear in histories of literature, and their works are set to be studied for school examinations. Austen, Dickens, Fielding, and Thackeray, are examples of authors of classical fiction.

Standard fiction is reasonably well written, but is generally without the staying power of classical fiction. A number of works of standard fiction will become in time, however, classics. The authors of standard fiction are sometimes well-known writers such as Kingsley Amis and Howard Spring, but on the whole their names are unknown to the average reader.

Light fiction is not easily separated from some standard fiction, except that it may be considered to aim more at entertaining readers. It can be compared, I suppose, to BBC Radio 2. As many readers have a preference for a particular type of light fiction, such as detective stories, romances, or westerns, a number of libraries shelf each type all together in one place. Agatha Christie, Netta Muskett, Zane Grey, are respectively typical authors of the three types of light fiction mentioned.

Light fiction of low quality, poorly written and even more poorly printed, is known as pulp fiction. This type of book is not stocked by libraries.

Non-fiction

Non-fiction books deal with facts, with people, places and things that exist, or have existed. It is often thought that the job of fiction is to entertain, the job of non-fiction to inform, but this distinction is a very rough one indeed. Many non-fiction books are written primarily to entertain, and not a few novels aim at putting before readers certain points of view. There are five types of non-fiction books that may be distinguished. After each type has been considered, two examples of that type from the subject field of archaeology are given. The five types are popular non-fiction, textbooks, standard works, monographs, and quick-reference books.

The popular non-fiction book sets out to entertain, though it may set out to give readers considerable information as well. For this reason popular non-fiction books are often written by authors who can write in an interesting fashion, rather than by experts.

Examples:

> CERAM, C. W. *Gods, graves, and scholars: the story of archaeology*
> WOOLLEY, SIR L. *Digging up the past*

It is obvious what the textbook sets out to do. Though most textbooks are written for students who have a teacher, there are textbooks designed for people trying to learn a subject without outside help. Textbooks will be simply written, accurate, well indexed, and they may contain examination questions and hints for students.

Examples:

> BRADE-BIRKS, S. G. *Teach yourself archaeology*
> MACALLISTER, R. A. S. *Textbook of European archaeology*

Standard works are carefully written by experts. They give as comprehensive a picture of their subject as possible, and are unbiased, accurate, well indexed, and with at least a select bibliography. Some advanced textbooks have become so well accepted by those who use them that they may also be considered to be standard works.

Examples:

> POWELL, T. G. E. *The Celts* (Ancient people and places series)
> WHEELER, SIR M. *Archaeology from the earth*

Monographs are written by experts for experts. They may contain the results of research and they will certainly contain specialized knowledge. They will be well equipped with indexes, glossary, bibliography, etc. New discoveries on a subject are normally first reported in articles in periodicals. If important enough, they are subsequently published in the form of a monograph. In due course a summary of the knowledge in the monograph will be incorporated into the standard works on the subject, and, if appropriate, into textbooks and popular works.

Examples:

DANIEL, G. *The prehistoric chamber tombs of England and Wales*

BEAZLEY, SIR J. D. *Etruscan vase painting* (Oxford monographs on classical archaeology)

Quick-reference books were briefly described in a previous chapter. They are fundamentally different from the other four types of non-fiction books, as they are not meant to be read as a whole but just to be dipped into. They are in great demand in libraries, and of considerable value when odd items of information are wanted quickly. They will be treated at length in the next chapter.

Examples:

COTTRELL, L., editor. *Concise encyclopaedia of archaeology.*

Who was who in Egyptology: a biographical index of Egyptologists

HOW TO JUDGE A BOOK

The quality of a book can be quickly judged by examining several factors. These factors will vary, depending on the type of book under consideration, but the following guide to them will generally prove helpful.

Fiction

Generally speaking a work of fiction has fewer Preliminaries than a non-fiction book, and possibly no Subsidiaries at all. This means that except for the information on the book jacket there is little to look for, short of dipping into the book itself. In a few fiction books, however, a summary of the plot is given on the half-title page of the book. Most help can be obtained by considering author, title, and publisher.

Author. The questions to ask about the author are: What else has he written? Do his books fall into any particular branch of fiction writing, such as historical novels? Does he aim to provide a story, to create characters, or to tackle a problem of some kind?

Title. The title of the book may be of help, but it must be admitted that the titles of novels are notoriously misleading.

Publisher. The name of the publisher is of particular note. In light fiction, for example, a Mills & Boon book will usually be a romance. If the book belongs to a publisher's series, such as Hutchinson's 'Crime Club', the title of the series is invariably helpful.

Non-fiction

The examination of non-fiction books is liable to take longer than that of fiction books as there are more points for which to look. These have been divided up under five headings, authors, subject matter, treatment, production, and date.

Author. The questions to ask about the author are: Is he an expert on the subject of the book? What kind of a reputation does he have? Can he write in simple language? Has he any pet theories? What else has he written? These questions can usually be answered at least to some extent by reading the book jacket and examining the Preliminaries.

Subject matter. The subject matter of the book is more difficult to assess, although some indication of it will often be given by the title. The reader should scan the book jacket and Preliminaries and glance through its pages if a little is known about the subject of the book. These measures should reveal the accuracy and up-to-dateness of the subject matter, and how comprehensively the subject is covered. They should also reveal whether the matter is largely drawn from other books, or is mainly the result of the author's own research.

Treatment. The treatment of the subject matter should be considered in the light of the five types of non-fiction books previously discussed as the divisions – popular works, textbooks, standard works, monographs, and quick-reference books – were obtained by classing books according to the way they treated their subject matter.

Production. The way a non-fiction book has been produced can make a great deal of difference to it. A full and accurate index is usually necessary, and this should be tested; also a bibliography. Adequate diagrams, maps, graphs, and other illustrative material should be included. The print should be large enough to read without strain. Of course, this applies also to works of fiction. Two other points best considered under this heading concern publisher and series. The name of the publisher may be of considerable importance as many firms have linked their names with particular subjects, or with particular types of books. Admittedly a knowledge of the book world is necessary fully to judge the publisher, but generally speaking the better the whole production of the book, the more the publisher can be relied upon. If the book belongs to a series, e.g. Collins' 'New Naturalist series', then this is of help in judging, as the standard of a series of books is usually fairly constant.

Date. Where other things are equal, the date decides. That statement is roughly true for the details of editions, etc. on the back of the title-page, not forgetting the date of copyright, can be easily ascertained, and are very important as most fields of knowledge are changing rapidly.

The next section of this chapter, though entitled 'Choosing which books to read', will mention many sources that can be tried to confirm a judgement on a book as well as to aid choosing one.

CHOOSING WHICH BOOKS TO READ

The final decision as to whether to read a book or not can only be taken when the book is actually in the hands of the reader. But there is not time to examine all the books on the shelves of libraries; in any case there will usually be a fair proportion of the stock on loan, and therefore not available for examination. So the reader must use ways that exist to enable him to take the advice of other people with expert knowledge who have examined the book. Three ways will be considered: using book reviews, using book-lists, and using certain reference books. They are not the only sources of information and advice open to readers, but they are authoritative sources.

Book reviews

Reviews of books vary from a few lines to whole articles. They are very popular with readers and surveys of readers have shown that they exert a considerable influence. Virtually every newspaper and periodical publishes a few book reviews from time to time. In specialized periodicals, such as *Nature*, the reviews are of course confined to appropriate specialist books, but in general newspapers and periodicals the reviews are of books of general interest. The Sunday newspapers, the *Sunday Times*, the *Observer* and the *Sunday Telegraph*, and the weekly periodicals, the *Listener*, the *New Statesman*, and the *Spectator*, are particularly noted for their reviews. A few periodicals devote most of their pages to book reviews, they are, among others:

Books and Bookmen. This is a well-illustrated monthly periodical that devotes about half of its pages to book reviews, and the rest to articles on literary topics and personalities, together with news about the book world. It probably reviews a wider range of fiction than any other periodical. A noteworthy feature is its 'Book Guide' which gives brief details under subject headings of recent books of general interest. There is also a similar paperback guide.

British Book News. In the order of the main classes of the Dewey classification scheme, *British Book News* briefly reviews each month the most important books on all subjects, including highly technical works, which are not reviewed by any other general reviewing source. It also includes an article dealing with the books on a particular subject, and a list of forthcoming books of all subjects.

Saturday Review of Literature. The United States publication that is of most interest to general readers on both sides of the Atlantic.

Times Literary Supplement. Every week the *Times Literary Supplement* reviews books and comments on other books in its 'Books received' section. It contains comparatively few articles. Its reviews are not signed.

Before passing on to book-lists, another American publication worthy of mention is the *Book Review Digest*. This periodical reviews book reviews. Under any particular book there are references to the reviews of that book in general English and American periodicals, including quotations from the reviews. Since 1965 it has been complemented by the *Book Review Index*, which is also American.

Book-lists

Reviews are of great help to readers, but they have one great drawback – they are only concerned with recently published books. This is where book-lists score, as they comment upon books on a particular subject, without much regard for when they were first published. There are book-lists, however, that are without comments. These are still of help as the books they list are restricted to the best books on the subject. From this point on, the word book-list will often be compared with the word bibliography. The two words are often used to mean the same thing, a list of books, but a clear distinction is now being drawn between them in these pages. A book-list is a select list of books on a subject, commonly with annotations; a bibliography is a virtually complete list of all the books on a subject. A book-list helps us choose what books we want to read, a bibliography helps us to find what books exist. Book-lists only are dealt with in this chapter; bibliographies, as they are of more interest to readers beginning research than to readers choosing books, in Chapter 6. Book-lists generally take one of three forms: an ordinary book, a series of pamphlets, or an article in a periodical. Looking first at book-lists that take the form of a book, five are of note.

COURTNEY, W. F. *The Reader's Adviser*. 11th ed. New York, Bowker, 1968–9. 2v. This is an American publication, particularly valuable for its comments on works of literary merit in every subject.

HOPPÉ, A. J. *Reader's Guide to Everyman's Library*. Rev. ed. Dent, 1966. Describes the 1,000 volumes in the publisher's famous series.

SMITH, F. S. *An English Library: an annotated list of classics and standard books*. New ed. Deutsch, 1963.

SMITH, F. S. *What Shall I Read Next: a personal selection of twentieth century English books*. Published for the National Book

League by Cambridge University Press, 1953. Complements the author's other work.

WILLIAMS, SIR W. E. *The Reader's Guide*. Penguin, 1960. Within this book there are eighteen short articles, each followed by an annotated book-list. The subjects range from 'Archaeology' to 'Science', and each section has been compiled by an expert.

There is also a series of books of note, the *Readers' Guide* series, published by Bingley. The annotations are in narrative form in this series, which includes titles on such subjects as *Railways* and the *Theatre*.

Passing on to book-lists that take the form of a series of pamphlets, two series may be noted.

LIBRARY ASSOCIATION. COUNTY LIBRARIES SECTION. *Reader's guides*. Listing the most important books on subjects such as *Architecture* or *Local history* these guides are of general interest. They are not annotated.

NATIONAL BOOK LEAGUE. *Book-lists*. These cover subjects in the same manner as the previous guides, but books are often commented upon. Recent titles have included *Careers*, *Teaching Reading*, and *Agriculture*.

Book-lists in the form of periodical articles can be found in many places, but the regular series found in the already noted *British Book News* is of especial value.

It has been shown that most book-lists are concerned with selecting the best books on a subject. There are, however, two special types of book-lists, one of which is concerned with recent books, the other with books which are shortly to be published. The restricted definition that was placed on the word book-list is stretched a little in order to include these two types.

Many libraries publish a list of their recent additions. This will often be published at monthly intervals and copies will be displayed for readers to take home. The list sometimes forms part of the library's magazine. (Such a magazine may also include articles that are virtually book-lists.)

The second special type of book-list is the publisher's catalogue. Book publishers produce every so often pamphlets describing the books they will shortly be publishing. Most publishers will send interested readers copies of their catalogues free of charge.

Reference Books

As well as reviews and book-lists, several reference books are useful to readers when choosing which books to read. Four reference books will be described, but there are others, most of them of a more specialized nature, such as the catalogue of the British Drama League, an indispensable guide to readers selecting plays.

ENSER, A. G. S. *Filmed Books and Plays: a list of books and plays from which films have been made.* Rev. ed. Deutsch, 1971. This lists those books made into films up to 1969. Where the title of the film differs from that of the book, this is indicated.

Cumulated Fiction Index. Association of Assistant Librarians. Covering novels published in this country since 1945, this is an extremely valuable work. It indexes the subject of each so that the reader requiring works of fiction to do, for example, with nursing, will find them listed together under that heading. The two basic volumes, which cover 1945–59 and 1960–69 respectively, are supplemented by annual volumes, the first, covering 1970, being published in 1971.

GARDNER, F. M. *Sequels.* 5th ed. Association of Assistant Librarians, 1967. Another extremely useful work, this reference book guides readers who wish to read in order such series of novels as the 'Whiteoaks' series by Mazo de la Roche, or the Herries saga by Hugh Walpole. A few non-fiction series and a few series of books for children are included, as are some books linked together just by certain characters.

SAMPSON, G. *Concise Cambridge History of English Literature.* 3rd ed. Cambridge University Press, 1970. There are several good guides to English literature, all of which are of help when choosing what classics to read. I have chosen this one as I have always found it of value.

The various aids to choosing books that have been described or mentioned will be available to readers in most libraries, though they will probably be for reference only. In libraries on specialized subjects more specialized guides that have not been mentioned will be in greatest demand.

About periodicals

Before concluding this chapter, some remarks are called for on
the subject of periodicals. Periodicals form an important part of
the stock of most libraries, and make a vital contribution towards the work of those libraries. This contribution is not as
well appreciated as it might be. The reason is simply explained.
The word periodicals automatically brings to mind the counter
of a newsagent's shop where, forming a rich variety of colour,
are copies of *Punch, Woman, Reveille*, and other similar publications. Such titles are rightly associated with relaxation, with
passing the time on a railway journey or in a doctor's waiting
room. The contents of periodicals are not therefore associated
with serious reading. But the contents of the majority of
periodicals that are published bear little resemblance to the
contents of these popular magazines. They are periodicals like
the *Engineer*, the *Accountant* and the *Museum's Journal* and contain the latest facts and opinions about the subjects with which
they deal. It is primarily because this is so that they are indispensable to readers, especially those readers whose needs are
considered in the next two chapters (that is those seeking
information or beginning research).

In most fields of knowledge advances are constantly being
made and it is only by constant reading of the appropriate
periodicals that it is possible to keep up to date with those
advances. (It has been estimated that information is two years
old before it is to be found in books.) But periodicals are also
stocked by libraries because much of the material which is
packed between their covers will never be found in books.
This may be because the material deals with research of a
highly specialized nature, or just because it is not suitable for
transfer to book form. Periodicals, it should be remembered,
besides featuring articles, reports, and news items, contain such
sections as 'Letters to the Editor' and 'Answers to Queries' and,
of course, advertisements. These special sections of periodicals
are of considerable importance.

So far in this part, a distinction has been drawn between
popular periodicals and those of a more serious nature. However, librarians usually divide periodicals in another way.

They divide them into the three groups: trade periodicals, learned society periodicals, and house journals.

Trade periodicals are produced by commercial publishers, and so, of course, their sales need to show a profit. It is the Trade periodical that is available from newsagents. All the periodicals that aim at giving pleasure as well as a large proportion of the more serious periodicals come into this category. Newspapers, by the way, belong to this group.

Learned society periodicals are published by societies, associations and institutions such as the Royal Meteorological Society and the Textile Institute. They aim principally at serving the members of the society, etc., and they are not published for profit. Libraries sometimes join the appropriate bodies in order to obtain their periodicals, but often the publications are available to non-members on payment of an annual subscription. Learned society periodicals are not usually to be seen in newsagents shops, neither are house journals.

House journals, which form the third and smallest group, are the periodicals produced by firms for either the information of their staff or their customers, or perhaps of both at the same time. They vary considerably in content, some including little more than staff gossip whilst others, such as the *Esso Magazine* and the *Midland Bank Review* include serious articles of a high quality and wide appeal. A selection of the more important house journals can be seen in many libraries.

Periodicals have been divided in the above way in order to illustrate the complexities of the world of periodical publication and, at the same time, reveal the various types of periodicals available to a reader interested in a particular subject. It is now time to consider briefly the actual obtaining of knowledge from periodicals. This topic is further considered in the next chapter under the heading 'Periodical Indexes and Abstracts'.

Periodicals are, on the whole, more difficult to consult than books. To begin with, the contents page for any particular issue may be hidden by pages of advertisements. Secondly, individual issues of periodicals have no indexes (though most serious periodicals publish an index once or twice a year). This often results in a third difficulty. Unless the exact issue of the periodical containing the required information is known, a hunt must be made through a large number of issues. This can be a formidable task, particularly if the periodical is published every week. But though there are difficulties to be faced when consulting periodicals, the required information having been found, the following points should be borne in mind. If a personal copy is wanted of the relevant pages, one can probably be photocopied for you by the library. Alternatively, if it is a whole article that is wanted, it may be possible to purchase an offprint of it. This is the name given to a copy of the article reprinted in the form of a pamphlet. It may, of course, even be possible to purchase a copy of the required issue of the periodical.

If you find that the library you are in does not have the periodical you require, it is possible to find out libraries that do, by referring to what are called Union lists of periodicals. The most important is the *British Union Catalogue of Periodicals*. There are also reference books that can help you find what periodicals exist on a particular subject. Such works, of which *Willing's Press Guide* is a good example, also give brief details about each periodical they list.

The subject of periodicals has been only introduced in this chapter. It is hoped, however, that sufficient information has been given to enable the periodicals that libraries possess to be used more fully and more efficiently.

BOOKS FOR FURTHER STUDY

DAVINSON, D. E. *The Periodicals Collection*. Deutsch, 1969.
The opening parts will be of most value to the non-librarian.
DE LEEUW, E. and M. *Read Better, Read Faster*. Penguin, 1968.
A course in efficient reading that can be recommended.
HARLEY, E. S. and HAMPDEN, J. *Books: from Papyrus to Paperback*. Methuen, 1964.

Chapter 5
Special needs
1 – Seeking information

Libraries as centres of information

The average person thinks of a library as a place from which he may borrow books, rather than a place from which he can obtain information. As a result, the importance of libraries as centres of information is not fully appreciated. The man in the street thinks of post offices and policemen, not of libraries, when he is stuck for facts. Yet libraries are, on the whole, far superior to other information sources. Libraries on specialized subjects may not be able to give much information on subjects other than their own, but most libraries are general enough in scope to be able to give information on virtually every subject. The reason why libraries are unrivalled as centres of information is quite obvious, for nearly all information finds its way into print. The amount of information contained in even a small library is staggering, but should the information required not be available the library staff will contact or suggest other possible sources.

Many readers who want to know something and don't wish to waste any time looking for it take their problem straight away to a member of the library staff. Other readers only do this after they have hunted high and low without success. It cannot be too highly stressed that if you want information and are a bit doubtful as to where to find it, don't waste time, but ask the staff to help you at once. Tell them exactly what you want and, if possible, why you want it. It is surprising how many readers only vaguely state what they require. I was asked on one occasion for a map of Lancashire. By questioning the person, I eventually discovered that what he wanted was a street plan of Manchester. If you know in which book the information is contained, and only wish to know where to find that book in the library, it is still best to say exactly what you require, as well as giving the title of the book you are looking for, because the library may not have the book and yet may have the necessary information in some other source. The advice to state your reasons for requiring the information is given because such background knowledge is of considerable value to the staff when evaluating any facts they unearth.

How to search for information

Many people regularly have to find out similar items of information such as telephone numbers. They will not find this difficult as, by virtue of their experience, they will have found out the best books in which to look for such information. Other people have to unearth items of information only occasionally; they may find this difficult as they probably do not know the best books to consult. Later in this chapter the most useful books for giving information will be considered. But first some suggestions must be made as to what to do when there is no obvious source that will yield the required information. On such occasions an organized hunt is called for. The following search routine is that used by librarians, but it can be followed almost as successfully by readers provided they know their way round the library. Examples of questions, the answers to which I have to hunt out, are: Which dog won the Waterloo Cup in 1868? What is the highest temperature regularly recorded at Lagos, Nigeria? How much traffic uses the Mersey Tunnel? What are the production figures for book matches in the United States? Where is the island of Daz, and what is known about it? The following plan of campaign must be taken as a general and not as an invariable guide. It should also be realized that there are a few questions to which it is impossible to find an answer.

General Quick-Reference Books should be tried first. The encyclopaedias, yearbooks, and the like, that cover all knowledge, are the most used group of books in libraries, as from them a large proportion of inquiries can be answered. No library can afford to be without the *Encyclopaedia Britannica, Whitaker's Almanack,* and similar general quick-reference books.

Quick-Reference Books on Individual Subjects. Most quick-reference books cover only a limited field of knowledge, perhaps biography, like *Who's Who*, or music, like Grove's *Dictionary of Music and Musicians*, or engineering, like Kemp's *Engineers' Pocket Book*. Questions that cannot be answered by general quick-reference books can usually be answered from the quick-reference books covering the appropriate subject. It is because quick-reference books are so useful that the last section of this chapter is devoted entirely to them.

Standard Works. When quick-reference books fail, the search must be continued, and the standard works on the subject of the problem should next be consulted. They will cover the subject in greater detail than the quick-reference books, though they will normally be less easy to use.

Monographs. If a deeper delving into the subject is necessary, monographs must be consulted. They will usually only be needed if the query is obscure as well as elusive.

Periodicals. The periodicals taken by the library should next be consulted. Information concerning periodicals and their importance was given in detail in the last chapter.

Pamphlets. If not shelved with the book stock, or with the clippings, but by themselves, these should be examined next.

Clippings. The library's file of newspaper and periodical clippings will be the best source of up-to-date information in the library. If the pamphlets are filed with the clippings, they will of course not be consulted till this stage in the search. For some items of information the clippings should be examined right at the start of the hunt, before even the quick-reference books.

Catalogue. There is a great deal to be said for consulting the catalogue of the library before beginning the search. However, if the whereabouts in the library of material on the subject is known, consulting the catalogue can be left to this point. It will probably reveal material that has so far been overlooked because it is shelved with another subject, or because it is shelved in reserve.

Staff. After any additional suggestions thrown up by the catalogue have been exhausted, the staff of the library should be consulted. Although a seemingly comprehensive search has been carried out by the reader, approaching the staff is never a waste of time. The staff can often find relevant material that the reader has missed, or be useful in other ways. Of course, the reader must tell the staff where he has looked, so that the staff will not look there again. The staff may have special information files that they have compiled, and unearth the needed item in them. They may contact outside libraries or organizations there and then, and obtain the answer from them. At the least they will suggest outside bodies and individuals that the reader should contact in his search. There is also one other purpose asking the staff may serve. It may reveal that the question just cannot be answered.

Quick-reference books

In the last section, quick-reference books were divided up into two categories, general quick-reference books, and quick-reference books on individual subjects. In this section quick-reference books are divided up in a different way, as the aim is to show the various kinds of information they contain. The six main classes of quick-reference books revealed by this division are dictionaries; encyclopaedias; maps, atlases and gazetteers; periodical indexes and abstracts; timetables; and, yearbooks and directories.

Dictionaries. The dictionary is the most common and familiar of all quick-reference books. It arranges words in alphabetical order, and is to be consulted not only when it is necessary to check the meaning of a particular word but also when the spelling or pronunciation of the word is in doubt. Some dictionaries, however, give further information, such as the origin and history of the word. Indeed it is sometimes difficult to decide whether a book is a dictionary or an encyclopaedia, so much information is given. It should be noted that some books, such as Grove's *Dictionary of Music and Musicians*, in spite of their titles, are without a doubt encyclopaedias, for they consist of articles not of definitions. They are given the name of dictionaries because their contents are arranged like a dictionary, in alphabetical order.

The most famous English dictionary is the *Oxford English Dictionary*, which runs to thirteen volumes (including the supplement). It defines nearly half a million words, and so is most likely to include any word that is wanted. The quality of its definitions is such that they are accepted as the standard definitions of words. Its examples of the use of words down the ages is another of its unrivalled features. The example below is one of the quotations given under the word 'Pestilence':

1539 Bible (Great) Ps. xc [i] 6. The pestilence that walketh in darkness.

However, for most purposes a less bulky dictionary is adequate. There are various abridgements of the *Oxford English Dictionary*, which, of course, can be relied upon, but so can several other dictionaries, such as *Chambers's Twentieth Century Dictionary*. These dictionaries, as well as being easy to handle, include words that have come into use since the publication of the great *Oxford English Dictionary*. They may also include useful supplementary features such as lists of common foreign phrases, boys' and girls' Christian names, and the more common abbreviations.

Supplementing the dictionaries proper, there will be found a number of other quick-reference books, all dealing with words, and these will be found alongside the main language dictionaries in libraries. Amongst the most useful of them are Partridge's *Dictionary of Slang*, for words not respectable enough for the average dictionary, Brewer's *Dictionary of Phrase and Fable*, for the meaning of mythological and similar words and phrases; and Roget's *Thesaurus*, which gives under a word all the other words of similar meaning and all the words that mean the opposite.

Supplementing the general language dictionaries in another way are the books that deal only with the words of one particular subject, such as medicine or engineering. These subject dictionaries are mainly confined to the scientific and technical

4

fields. *Chambers's Dictionary of Science and Technology* is an example that will be found in most libraries. These subject dictionaries will be shelved with the quick-reference books on the appropriate subject, and not with the other dictionaries.

So far all the dictionaries considered have to do with English words, but libraries also stock a selection of dictionaries of foreign languages and of translating dictionaries. Translating dictionaries give the word in English, followed by its equivalent in a foreign language. The series of such dictionaries published by the firm of Cassell will be found to meet most needs.

Before concluding these paragraphs on dictionaries, two other types of quick-reference books need to be touched on. These are not perhaps dictionaries in the strict sense of the word, but they are most appropriately considered at this point. The first type is dictionaries of quotations. If a quotation on a particular subject, or the author of a certain quotation, or the exact words of a quotation that cannot quite be remembered, are required, these books will provide the answer. Most libraries will have a selection of them, and the *Oxford Dictionary of Quotations* should be tried first. The second type is the concordance. A concordance is similar to a book of quotations, but its scope is limited to the words of a single book, or perhaps the work of a single author. The other way in which it differs from a book of quotations is that it indexes not just the most quoted passages, but every word and phrase. It indicates, against each word it indexes, the places where that word is to be found in the book. The concordance most often found in libraries is Cruden's *Complete Concordance to the Old and New Testaments*. The *Oxford Dictionary of Quotations* gives the places in the Bible where frequently quoted phrases, such as 'Ye are the salt of the earth' (Matthew, ch. 5, verse 13) appear. Cruden's *Concordance* reveals that the word 'salt' appears twenty-six times in the Bible, and one of its references runs:

'Mt. 5. 13. Ye are the s. of the earth, but if the s.'

Encyclopaedias. Encyclopaedias differ from dictionaries in that they consist of a series of articles rather than a series of words. The articles vary in length from a few lines to several pages and are written by experts. In many encyclopaedias the names or the initials of the authors appear at the end of the articles.

Encyclopaedias will answer all questions of general information such as: What is the height of Mount Everest? Who were the Luddites? Where is the island of Saint Helena? They will also give the basic facts on subjects from Alchemy to Zoology. They are, in addition, useful because they contain illustrations, and because they often suggest the books to study if further information is required. If you require information on a subject of which you know little, an encyclopaedia will give you an outline of the subject, and enable you to continue your search with a clearer mind.

The greatest encyclopaedia and also the oldest, as its first edition was published between 1768 and 1771, is the *Encyclopaedia Britannica* (25 volumes, including index and atlas). One of the difficulties that the *Encyclopaedia Britannica* (and the other large encyclopaedias) has to face is how to keep its contents up to date. An encyclopaedia that is not up to date is a poor encyclopaedia, yet revising such massive works is not easy. As a result, the *Encyclopaedia Britannica*, as well as gradually revising its contents a little at a time, supplements its main volumes by publishing each year a *Britannica Book of the Year*.

Similar, though rather smaller encyclopaedias are also available in libraries, and these will frequently be complementary to the *Encyclopaedia Britannica* in some way. The best of them are *Chambers's Encyclopaedia* (15 volumes) and the *Oxford Junior Encyclopaedia* (13 volumes). This last is virtually an adult encyclopaedia in spite of its name. At the other end of the scale there are useful one-volume encyclopaedias of which the best known is *Pear's Cyclopaedia*. Although some of these small encyclopaedias will be found in libraries, they are mainly designed to be used in the home.

The articles in encyclopaedias are usually arranged in one alphabetical sequence, the *Oxford Junior Encyclopaedia* being one of the few exceptions to this rule, but the larger ones will also have an index to make finding the required information easier. This index, which will be found at the end of the last volume, can be most useful as the subject on which the reader is seeking information may not have an article to itself but be included in another article, or there may be information on a subject in several different places in the encyclopaedia. The index will reveal both these points.

So far, only encyclopaedias covering all branches of know-ledge have been considered, but the majority of encyclopaedias deal only with a single branch of knowledge. Grove's *Dictionary of Music and Musicians* is a subject encyclopaedia that has al-ready been mentioned, others are Hasting's *Encyclopaedia of Religion and Ethics,* Kingzett's *Chemical Encyclopaedia,* and *Chambers's Cyclopaedia of English Literature.*

It has been noted that some encyclopaedias call themselves dictionaries. A few encyclopaedias have other names. *The Oxford Companion to English Literature* is the best known of a series of 'companions' published by the Oxford University Press. The only difference that can be drawn between a companion and an encyclopaedia is that the companion treats subjects in a more homely manner, hence its name. The encyclopaedias that concern themselves with places and call themselves gazetteers will not be dealt with at this point but under the next heading, 'Maps, Atlases, and Gazetteers'.

One type of encyclopaedia remains to be considered, the kind that deals with persons. Such encyclopaedias are given the name of biographical dictionaries.

Details about people are given of course in general encyclo-paedias, but biographical dictionaries are more comprehensive. They usually observe one restriction, however, that is not to be found in general encyclopaedias dealing either with the living or with the dead. If they deal with the living, they confine themselves to facts; if with the dead, comments are included. *Who's Who* is the best guide to the living, and it will be found in virtually all libraries. The information it gives about the 20,000 or so persons within its pages includes address, education, posts held, books written, even hobbies. The *Dictionary of National Biography* is without a rival in providing information about British subjects who are no longer alive.

Maps, Atlases, and Gazetteers. Atlases are collections of maps, combined with an index to the maps. Single maps, usually called sheet maps, though not themselves quick-reference books, will be considered together with atlases. Atlases are in common use in schools as well as in libraries, for locating places and also for confirming the existence of places. School atlases are normally a different shape from the average book, but quite a handy size all the same. Library atlases are rather larger in every way than school atlases; the most important library atlas has a page area six times that of an ordinary book. This is *The Times Atlas of the World*, which is up to date, accurate, and goes into considerable detail, giving street plans of the centres of the most important towns of the world. School atlases deal with countries from a general geographical point of view, while some library atlases deal instead with a more specialized aspect of a country or countries. An example of this kind of atlas is the *Oxford Economic Atlas of the World*. The purpose of this atlas is to show the economic resources of countries, what they grow, what they manufacture, and their natural resources, such as coal and oil. The index to both general and specialized atlases is a vitally important part. This will give after each name the page and map number, and the latitude and longitude of the place. If, as is common practice, each map is divided up into squares to make reference easier, the index will also give the square number.

Sheet maps, unlike atlases, are not normally indexed, which makes them more difficult to use. They are, nonetheless, of great value, and the various series of sheet maps issued by the official British map-making body, the Ordnance Survey, are in constant use in libraries. The Ordnance Survey maps range from ones on which a mile is represented by a $\frac{1}{20}$ inch, to maps which allow each mile fifty inches. The smaller scale maps are used by motorists and hikers, the larger scale ones by surveyors and town planners. The series with the largest scale that covers the whole country is the six inch to the mile. This series, which gives the names of streets, will be found complete in the large reference libraries. The Ordnance Survey maps, like other aspects of our life, are to go metric. A particular form of sheet maps are town plans. Unlike most other sheet maps, these usually include an index, as their purpose is to help find streets, etc.

A gazetteer gives the latitude and longitude of places, together with a brief description of them. For example, if the reference is to a town, the population and industries of the town will be noted as well as the distance of the town from other landmarks. Gazetteers and maps supplement each other, as from the description of a place given in a gazetteer it can be found on a map. Together, they supply sufficient geographical information for most purposes. The most important gazetteers are, for the world, the *Columbia Lippincott Gazetteer of the World*, and, for Great Britain, *Bartholomew's Survey Gazetteer of the British Isles*.

Periodical Indexes and Abstracts. It was stated in the last chapter that periodicals are not easy to search for information. Periodical indexes make reference much easier. They enable articles on a particular subject, and usually articles by a particular author or with a given title, to be quickly traced. There are two types of periodical index. The first indexes just a single periodical. It may be like the index to a book and be included at the back of each issue of the periodical, but more often it is issued separately at fixed intervals, perhaps once a year, and includes entries for articles appearing over the whole period. Most scholarly periodicals publish such indexes. When libraries keep and bind these periodicals into volumes they usually bind the issues in such a way that there is an index to each bound volume. A few newspapers issue indexes and these indexes, owing to the vast amount of information contained in a newspaper, are very valuable. Unfortunately only one national newspaper in this country, *The Times*, publishes an index.

The second type of periodical index covers a number of periodicals over a short period. It usually takes a hundred or more periodicals dealing with a particular branch of knowledge, and, if the index appears at monthly intervals, indexes the contents of the periodicals during the previous month. To aid reference, many indexes cumulate, that is they produce from time to time issues that give the contents of several numbers of the index. Within the index the subjects covered will be listed alphabetically, and, under each, there will be given details of appropriate articles. The most famous series of periodical indexes is published by the United States firm of H. W. Wilson & Co. Perhaps the most used index within this series is the *Applied Science and Technology Index* which covers several hundred periodicals on the subjects suggested by its title. Examples of questions that it will answer are: Where can I find some up-to-date information on steel technology in Russia? What articles

have there been recently on insulating materials? I recently
saw an article on abrasives but I have no idea in which
periodical I saw it. Can you find it? A British index of similar
scope began publication in 1962. Called the *British Technology
Index* and published each month by the Library Association,
it indexes by subject the contents of nearly 400 scientific and
technical periodicals. The Library Association began publication at the same time of a complementary but quarterly index,
the *British Humanities Index*. These two indexes, together with
the *British Education Index* (published by the Library Association
in conjunction with the English Institutes of Education),
enable the majority of important articles on all subjects that
appear in British periodicals to be traced.

A limitation on the usefulness of indexes to periodicals is that
few libraries take all the periodicals indexed by any one
periodical index. Useful references may therefore be found
which cannot be followed up, as the appropriate periodicals
are not available. This limitation is one of the reasons why a
number of libraries, particularly those belonging to industrial
firms, issue their own indexes to periodical articles which, of
course, include only periodicals taken by the library. This
disadvantage can also be partly overcome by the use of abstracts
of periodical articles. The only difference between these and
indexes is that abstracts include a summary of the contents of
the articles. By reading the summary of the article readers can
often tell whether or not they need to see the original article.
The most used abstracting journals are in the field of science
and technology; the most celebrated is the American *Chemical
Abstracts*. It is to be noted that certain specialized periodicals
devote a section of each of their issues to abstracts of interest to
their readers. The *Journal of the Science of Food and Agriculture*
is a typical example.

Timetables. Many people find timetables difficult to use. In fact,
they are not really difficult to understand once the funda-
mental principles governing them are appreciated. This
appreciation can only be gained by examining them closely.
When this has been done, it will be found they not only aid
travel from one place to another, but give details of geographical
distances, of half closing and market days, even of hotels.

Foreign timetables can also be used as rough and ready gazetteers. There are timetables for all of the four main means of travel: road, rail, sea, and air.

The majority of bus timetables are of a local nature, but most libraries, as well as stocking the appropriate local time-tables, will stock the National Bus Co. timetable. This gives details of the mainline bus services covering this country. For travelling by train, the series of regional timetables published by British Rail is most comprehensive and can be used with confidence. Timetables for sea and air travel, though not in so much demand, will also be found, at least in the larger libraries.

Yearbooks and Directories. Directories and yearbooks to some extent serve different purposes; they are being considered together as many directories contain yearbook information, and many yearbooks directory information. It is for this reason that publishers will be found to use the two words indiscriminately. Directories are more easily defined than year-books; they obviously exist to direct readers in some way. The three main questions they set out to answer are: Who lives at a stated address? What is the address of a particular person or place? and What firms (or persons) are there in a certain line of business?

There are three kinds of directories found on the shelves of libraries. The first kind is the local directory, which answers the above three questions so far as a particular town or locality is concerned. It is commonly assumed by members of the public that there are local directories covering the whole country. Unfortunately this is not so, as only for the large cities can a local directory be guaranteed and this may not be published every year. The local directory will usually be arranged in three sequences, the first listing alphabetically by street the householders within the street; the second listing the people of the town alphabetically by their surnames; and the third, classifying firms, etc. by their trade so that, for example, all the names of chimney sweeps in the area are conveniently gathered together. The trades in this third section will be arranged in alphabetical order. The second kind of directory, the trades directory, will have just two sequences; the sequence by street is omitted as the directory will cover the whole country. There are a large number of directories covering individual trades, such as *Skinner's Cotton Trade Directory* and *Ryland's Coal, Iron and Steel Trades Directory*; there are also a few directories which cover all trades. The most valuable of these is *Kelly's Manufacturers and Merchants Directory*. The third kind of directory is the telephone directory, which consists of a single sequence arranged alphabetically by the names of subscribers. However, there is a series of telephone directories that is arranged alphabetically by trade. These classified telephone directories are increasingly being bound in on yellow pages with the alphabetical local directory.

It has already been noted that yearbooks often contain some directory information. Another thing the two types of books have in common is that they both normally appear annually. On what points do they differ? The aims of yearbooks are far wider, their purpose being to give up-to-date information of every variety as simply as possible. They contain not only information usually found in directories but also information that is usually found in textbooks and standard works, dictionaries and encyclopaedias. They include addresses and biographies, weights and measures and statistics, definitions and abbreviations, the latest discoveries, and well-established facts. It is remarkable how many questions can be answered from yearbooks.

Nearly all yearbooks deal with a limited field of knowledge, but there are a few general yearbooks. The one of this general kind that librarians rate most highly is *Whitaker's Almanack*; indeed, it is generally agreed that no other book of its size is consulted so often and so successfully. To give some idea of the questions it will answer, I have listed below five questions that I have answered recently by reference to it: Can you give me a list of the winners of the Victoria Cross? On what day of the week did the 30th of November fall in 1892? What is the address of the Hospital Saturday Fund? Who is the member of parliament for Altrincham and Sale? What is the population of Peterborough?

The yearbooks that deal with a limited field of knowledge normally cover every variety of information in that field. Typical examples of such yearbooks are the *Municipal Yearbook,* the *Hospitals Yearbook* and the *Yearbook of Technical Education*. There are a few exceptions to this rule, however, which limit themselves to a single form of information about a subject, for example statistical information. Statistical yearbooks, surveying yearbooks and professional lists are the three types that may be noted. The name statistical yearbook is self-explanatory, but the names surveying yearbook and professional list need a word of explanation. Surveying yearbooks are so called because they survey the advances, discoveries and developments of the previous year, professional lists because they give the names of members of professions such as doctors, lawyers, architects. A quick-reference book, that is produced in a loose leaf form every week, is *Keesing's Contemporary Archives*. It is mentioned at this point, as it surveys current affairs throughout the world in a similar way to surveying yearbooks.

Before closing this section on Yearbooks and Directories, there is one further type of reference material to be considered, namely, voting lists. These are the official records on which the name of a person must appear if he or she wishes to vote at a national or local government election. Voting lists, or electoral registers as they are sometimes called, are invaluable as they are the only published record of the adult occupants, as opposed to householders, of houses. Arranged by street, they supplement the street section of local directories not only because they list virtually all inhabitants over eighteen years of age, but also because they cover the whole country and are often more up to date than directories as they are revised once a year. There is no official list of the inhabitants of an area arranged alphabetically by surname.

This chapter has dealt mainly with quick-reference books, and the value of them has been indicated. But if you are doubtful about the facts revealed by a quick-reference book, do not hesitate to consult another as a check. Quick-reference books do contain inaccuracies, and some books are more up to date than others.

Most libraries will contain the reference books described. However, they are only a sample of the vast number that are available. Further quick-reference books, including ones on specialized subjects, will be found described in the works listed for further study at the end of this chapter.

Reference books for the home

Quick-reference books are so useful that it is well worth while having a shelf of them at home. This will save you having to go to the library whenever you want to look things up, though you will still have to go there with your more difficult problems. I have therefore selected a few titles that could form the basis of your home reference library. I have used the term 'Reference books for the home' to head this section rather than 'Reference books for the personal library' because reference books in a house will be used by all in that home. You cannot keep them to yourself. The details given about each selected book include price (though this is subject to change) and a short annotation.

To make your home reference library as good as possible you will also need titles dealing with your own particular interests and with subjects like cookery, gardening and other home topics. (The titles suggested are all of very general interest and scope.) In addition, you will need works that give information on your own locality. You may already have the local telephone directory. A street map, a local guide book of some kind, and transport timetables, are all handy to have around.

ESSENTIAL TITLES

Concise Oxford Dictionary. 5th ed. Oxford University Press, 1965. £1.50.
A dictionary is a first buy and this dictionary is up to date and authoritative. If you prefer a dictionary that will act to some extent as an encyclopaedia the *Oxford Illustrated Dictionary*, with its entries for people and places, is worth considering.
Pear's Cyclopaedia. 80th ed. Pelham Books, 1971. £1.50.
Probably the best encyclopaedia to buy for the home as, in addition to the kind of information found in other small encyclopaedias, it contains sections devoted to such subjects as gardening, health, and cookery. It also includes a few pages of maps of the world. A one-volume encyclopaedia of more

conventional approach and arrangement is *Hutchinson's Twentieth Century Encyclopaedia*.

Oxford Home Atlas. 3rd ed. rev. Oxford University Press, 1969. £1.25.
There are many world atlases of about the same size as this one, but some are designed for school rather than home use. If you are being economical it is possible to make do with the atlas section in *Pear's*, but you will soon find you need the extra detail given by works like this atlas.

RECOMMENDED TITLES

These are simply listed in alphabetical order.

Brewer's Dictionary of Phrase and Fable. Rev. ed. Cassell, 1970. £3.
A mixture of an encyclopaedia and a dictionary of proverbs and phrases. Especially recommended to readers of literature and history.

Central Office of Information. *Britain 1972: An Official Handbook*. Annual. HMSO. £1.80.
Covers in fair detail most British institutions and many aspects of life in Britain today. Well designed and indexed.

Daily Mail Yearbook. Annual. Associated Newspapers Ltd. 35p.
Yearbooks date more quickly than most types of reference books, especially those that devote part of their contents to reviewing the previous year, as does this one. However, they are mines of miscellaneous information, and at 35p this publication is an economic and worthwhile purchase. *Whitaker's Almanack* is more comprehensive but costs £1.50 for the full text.

ELLIOTT, F. *Dictionary of Politics*. 6th ed. Penguin, 1969. 50p.
One of a series of reference books which are cheap yet sound, this work would be better entitled 'Encyclopaedia of world affairs'. Helps the understanding of those problems that seem to be constantly in the news.

Guinness Book of Records. Rev. ed. Guinness Superlatives, 1971. £1.05.
A well-known compilation that is eminently browsable and

provides the answers to those innumerable questions on the fastest, biggest and best. Many topics are covered, and sport, as you might expect, is particularly well covered.

Shell Guide to Britain. 2nd. ed. Ebury Press, 1969. £2.25.
Valuable for touring purposes, but just as good for armchair geography and travel. Is arranged as a quick-reference book and includes a map section.

BOOKS FOR FURTHER STUDY

BAGLEY, W. A. *Facts and How To Find Them.* 6th ed. Pitman, 1962.
LINDEN, W. O. *Books and Libraries.* Cassell, 1964.
Mainly a guide to reference books, both general and special.
WALFORD, A. J. and others. *Guide to Reference Material.* Revised ed.
Library Association, 1966–1970. 3v.
An annotated and authoritative guide to the best quick-reference books on all subjects.

Chapter 6
Special needs
2 – Beginning research

Libraries and research

Research may be defined as exact, patient and prolonged study. The word is often used to refer to finding out all there is to know about a subject; in this chapter it will be used more loosely to mean investigating a subject generally as opposed to searching for individual items of information. Research, though the word is most commonly used in scientific and industrial contexts, is being continually carried out in all fields of knowledge. On the whole, research may be considered to be of two kinds. The first has as its object the crossing of the frontiers of knowledge, it results in new inventions and discoveries; the second aims at drawing fresh conclusions from facts already known. The first kind of research is particularly important in science and technology, the second in history and sociology, but both kinds are necessary in every subject. Of course, research of both kinds can be carried out at more than one level. There is the full-scale research level, such as is reached by the writer of a thesis, and there is the limited research level of, for example, the school child working on a project. Now research, whether limited or full-scale, demands more than anything else knowledge of what facts and ideas are already known. Whatever the need of the research worker, some reservoir of knowledge has to be tapped. This is where libraries come in, as libraries are the largest of all reservoirs of knowledge. It has previously been shown that the primary function of the great reference libraries is to act as reservoirs of knowledge, but it should be remembered that the knowledge stored in most other kinds of libraries is sufficient to meet many research needs. A research worker will consult experts on the subject of his research, and in other ways, such as by laboratory experiments, try to increase his knowledge. But, on the whole, he will have to spend most of his time consulting what has been written on his subject. Only in this way can he make reasonably sure of the knowledge he has at his disposal.

Probably only people who have spent some time in their lives doing research of a fairly high standard can fully appreciate the research value of libraries. That they do appreciate their indebtedness to libraries can be seen by looking at the acknowledgements in many scholarly books. Such people may also acknowledge the help given them by library staff. Advice from library staff is needed by virtually all research workers, particularly at the start of the research project. And, generally speaking, the person carrying out limited research needs to ask for help as much as the full-scale research worker, though over a shorter period.

Readers beginning research should seek the help of library staff, and they should also be able to help themselves. There are two main ways research workers can help themselves. The first, of course, is by knowing how to use the library, or libraries, in which they are working. The second is by mastering certain research techniques. The rest of this chapter will be mainly concerned with some of these research techniques.

Research techniques

The word technique means practical skill in doing a job. Such skill comes principally from being taught the job properly. Those beginning research, as those tackling any other job, need to master the appropriate techniques. Three research techniques will be considered in this chapter. There are others, such as how to take notes from books, but they are outside the scope of this work. One or two helpful books on these other techniques are included in the 'Books for further study'. The three techniques to be considered I have entitled, 'Finding out what is known', 'Noting bibliographical information' and 'Understanding bibliographical references'.

FINDING OUT WHAT IS KNOWN

There are various possible approaches to the problem of finding out what is known about a subject. If the research is of a very limited nature, such as would be needed for school homework, and concerns a subject about which the investigator knows little, the first step should be to read what is written about the topic in an encyclopaedia. If the encyclopaedia does not contain sufficient information, then the next step should be to consult any books suggested for further reading in the encyclopaedia, or straight away to consult the library's catalogue and find out what books the library possesses on the subject.

The consultation of the library's catalogue should be the first step when the research is of a rather more comprehensive nature, such as would be needed in order to give a talk on a subject. How much material the catalogue will reveal will depend, of course, on the size and scope of the library. Two points should be borne in mind, however, or much material may be overlooked. The first is that material on the subject being investigated will be found also in books on related subjects. For example, if the subject of research is morris dancing, then the catalogue should be checked for what it contains on folk dancing, dancing in general, and on English customs. The second point is that the library may not have all its stock listed in its main catalogue. There may be a separate catalogue, for example, to the library's local collection. Indeed, there may be two main catalogues, one to the library's lending department, the other to its reference department. If no material is to be overlooked, therefore, several catalogues may have to be checked.

It should be remembered that the catalogues of a library normally only list material that has appeared as a separately published book or pamphlet. They exclude material on the subject that has appeared in periodical articles. And so, if this material is to be consulted, it must be located by some other means. It will have to be located, in fact, by using periodical indexes and abstracts (which were considered in the last chapter). Any relevant articles so located will then have to be checked against the library's stock of periodicals in order to find out if the library takes the required periodicals. It might be added here that research workers should realize that information on the subject they are investigating may be found too on maps, on illustrations, and in collections of newspaper clippings.

When the research is of a fairly high standard, an alternative first step to consulting the library's catalogue is to consult a guide to the literature of the appropriate subject. Such guides list, with comments, the most important contributions (in any form) to the study of the subject. Examples of such guides are Dyson's *Short guide to chemical literature* and Baron's *Bibliographical guide to the English educational system*.

If the research is of a comprehensive nature, the research worker may begin his work by compiling a bibliography of the material that he may need to consult. The material for his bibliography he will extract from printed bibliographies available for consultation in the library. The consultation of such bibliographies as are described at the end of this chapter will not only enable the research worker to discover what has already been written on the subject he is investigating, but also to find out whether another has already carried out the research he is proposing to do. A full-scale research programme that begins with the compilation of a bibliography consists altogether of the following five stages.

1. *Compiling the bibliography*

The details of the various relevant books, periodical articles,etc., that are traced through the library's bibliographies and catalogues will be noted down. They will form the raw material of the research workers own bibliography. Even material that is of doubtful relevance to the research in question should be noted. On examination, it may reveal important information. The technique of 'Noting bibliographical information' is a research technique in its own right, it is therefore considered separately later in this chapter.

2. *Arranging the bibliography*

The details of appropriate books, periodical articles and other material having been unearthed and noted, the next stage is to put the bibliography in some sort of order. The material can be placed under author in simple alphabetical order, but, generally speaking, this is not a very helpful arrangement. The whole point in compiling the bibliography is to aid the research worker in his task. A classified arrangement of the material under the aspects of the subject being investigated will better suit this need. The research worker may obtain ideas for his classification scheme from the arrangement of book classification schemes used by libraries. He may also obtain them from the arrangement of the bibliographies he has consulted. Generally speaking, it is not wise to classify material by its physical form, for example into books, periodicals, manuscripts, pamphlets, etc. Books on historical subjects lend themselves to being classified chronologically as well as by subject, and those on geographical subjects lend themselves to being classified partly by place. Bibliographies of authors will have to list the books by the author as well as those about him. Such bibliographies are therefore often arranged as follows: (a) collected editions of the author's works; (b) selections of the author's works; (c) editions of individual works; (d) works that were not published; (e) material about the author.

3. *Surveying the bibliography*

When the bibliography has been placed in a satisfactory order, this third stage can be started. The research worker will look through the material he has listed, and decide in what order he must examine it. If he has discovered a tremendous amount of material, he may decide to examine only a selection of the material on each aspect of his subject.

4. *Examining material*

This is the stage that will take the research worker most of his time. He will first need to trace where he can see the material that comprises his bibliography, and then, having tracked it down, he can examine it. Very often he will have to travel to libraries, as the material may not be available for borrowing. He may also invoke the help of inter-library schemes for borrowing books. The inter-lending scheme centred on the National Central Library was described in Chapter 2; through this and other inter-lending schemes a surprising amount of material can be borrowed.

5. *Compiling information*

As each item of material is examined, the relevant information it contains will be written down. At the same time a careful note of the source of the information will be made in case it is necessary to refer to it again, and so the research work can be presented fully documented. This noting of the sources of information demands virtually the same technique as is needed to compile a bibliography.

NOTING BIBLIOGRAPHICAL INFORMATION

The technique of noting bibliographical information, either when compiling a bibliography, or when writing down the sources from which information has been obtained, is based on cataloguing practice. It therefore follows, on the whole, the principles laid down in Chapter 3. The noting of bibliographical information can be carried out on the lines suggested without much difficulty when the research worker has the material in front of him, as he will normally have when he is noting his sources of information. But, at the compiling of the bibliography stage of his work, he will only have the details about the material given in the bibliographies to go on. He should decide exactly what he is going to note down about each book, and then aim at being consistent. If the printed bibliography does not give all the information he requires, he should leave blank spaces which can be filled up when he sees the material. The following points should be jotted down when noting books. More or fewer details may be copied if the worker desires, but the first five items should always be included. The details are: (a) author's surname in capital letters, followed by his Christian names or initials; (b) title, this may be abbreviated if long; (c) edition, if not the first; (d) publisher's name, and place of publication if thought necessary; (e) date of book; (f) number of volumes if more than one; (g) number of pages. If the book is illustrated, has a bibliography, or forms one of a series of books, these facts should be included.

Example:
   MANLEY, GORDON. *Climate and the British Scene.* Collins, 1952. 314 pp. Illus. (New Naturalist series)

If the material is an article in a periodical, the note made should give the following details: (a) author of article; (b) title of article; (c) name of periodical; (d) volume number, issue number, and date of issue of periodical; (e) pagination of article.

Example:
> POLLOCK, JOHN. Advertising To Sell Paper. *Paper and Print,* vol. 31, no. 4, Winter, 1959. pp. 87–88.

If the article is not in a periodical but forms part of a book, then the author and title of the article should be followed by the full details of the book.

Example:
> BROWN, IVOR. Drama. *Williams, Sir William Emrys.* The Reader's Guide. Penguin, 1960. pp. 113–141.

If it is not an article in a periodical, but a whole issue of a periodical that needs to be noted, then the details recorded should include the publisher of the periodical, and possibly the place of publication.

Example:
> BOOK DESIGN AND PRODUCTION. vol. 1, no. 3, Autumn, 1958. Printing News Ltd.

Three points need to be added to what has so far been laid down. When the last date in the book is the date the book was most recently reprinted, another date indicating accurately the age of the book's contents is called for. It should be possible to ascertain this date from the information given on the back of the title page. It can then be included in the description of the book as indicated in Chapter 3, e.g. 1948 (1960 repr.). The second point is that material belonging to a library will have a class number or similar device showing where it is shelved. It is useful if a note is also made of this. Thirdly, it is customary in printed books to make use of italic letters as above. In manuscripts these items should be underlined instead.

From the examples given it will be seen that certain abbreviations are used to shorten the description of material. The meaning of those in most common use is therefore set out. Abbreviations explained in Chapter 3 will be found among them.

bk. – book
bibliog. – bibliography
ch. – chapter
col. – column
ed. – edition or editor
f. or ff. – following
illus. – illustrated
l. – line (ll. – lines)
n. – note
no. – number

p. – page (pp. – pages)
par. – paragraph
pt. – part
rep. – reprint (repr. – reprinted)
rev. – revised
ser. – series
sect. – section
v. – verse (vv. – verses)
vol. – volume

It was mentioned in Chapter 3 that when a book is catalogued, the information on the title page should be copied exactly. In the same way, when noting bibliographical information it is customary to be exact. For example, when a page or volume number is written down, if the information given is in roman numerals it will be copied down in roman numerals. As roman numerals are not always easily understood the letters that comprise them are briefly explained. It should be noted that either capital letters or lowercase letters can be used to make them.

Basic Numerals
I – One
V – Five
X – Ten
L – Fifty
C – Hundred
D – Five hundred
M – Thousand

Examples of use
III – Three
IV – Four
VII – Seven
XXIX – Twenty-nine
LXVI – Sixty-six
MDCCCLXX – 1870
MCMLXI – 1961

UNDERSTANDING BIBLIOGRAPHICAL REFERENCES

It was stated in Chapter 4 that bibliographical references are normally placed alongside the author's notes. They are usually to be found therefore at the bottom of each page of text-matter. The author may refer to other books in the text, but it is customary to place in the text only some sign indicating that there is a reference to be found at the bottom of the page. References may be to other books on the subject that the author is considering; they may be to the sources from which the author has obtained his material; they may be to the place from which the author has taken quotations. They may also refer to other pages within the book where related information can be found.

It has been stated that the most common place for references is the foot of each page of the text, and this is certainly the most convenient place for them from the reader's point of view. References will sometimes be found instead, however, at the end of each chapter or even relegated to the Subsidiaries. No matter where they are placed, references will be linked by signs of some sort to the appropriate places in the text. These signs are usually small arabic numerals, ¹, ², ³, which the printer calls 'superiors' because of their elevated position, but they can also take the form of lower case letters, a, b, c, etc., or of printers' signs, *†‡ etc. References to other books will generally follow the pattern give under 'Noting bibliographical information' and give similar information to that found in library catalogues. It is quite common for fewer details to be given, however, and, when a book has once been referred to in full, only the title and relevant page number may be given in subsequent references. Indeed, it is customary, though not always convenient to the reader, to abbreviate references still further. This means that readers must know the meaning of certain terms. The following are the ones most likely to be met with.

(a) *Ibid* (or *Ib*.). This abbreviation is short for *ibidem*, which means 'in the same place'. It is used when there are several references following each other to a single book. The first reference will, of course, give the full details of the book; subsequent references just state *Ibid.*, e g.:

PHILLIPS, J. B. *Your God is too Small*, p. 27.
Ibid. p. 34.

(b) *Idem* (or *Id*.). This word, which means 'the same', is used when subsequent references are not to the same book, but to other books by the same author. The following example shows how it is used.

Idem. Letters to Young Churches. p. 155.

(c) *op. cit.* Short for *opera citato* which means 'in the work quoted', this abbreviation is used in a similar way to *ibid* except that it is always preceded by the appropriate author's name, e.g:

Jones. *op. cit.* p. 24.

It complements *ibid* for, as it gives the author's name, it can be used well away from the original full reference.

(d) *loc. cit.* Meaning 'in the place cited', this abbreviation usually occurs when a reference to an article in a periodical is followed by further references to the same article. A reference using *loc. cit.* will give the author's name but not usually a page number, e.g.:

William. loc. cit.

(e) *et sequens* (or *et seq.*). This means 'and the following' and can be used when the subject referred to occurs several times in the book in question. The first page on which the subject is mentioned is stated, but for the subsequent page numbers is substituted this particular phrase. e.g.:

MATTHEWS, L. H. *British Mammals*. Collins, 1952. p. 20 *et sequens*.

(f) *passim*. Sometimes the subject referred to is only dealt with in detail at one place in the book referred to, but is mentioned elsewhere in it. The word *passim*, which means 'here and there', is used to indicate this, e.g.:

PALMER, K. *Teach Yourself Music*. English Universities Press, 1950. p. 11 *passim*.

(g) *vide*. This word, which means 'see', may be used in a reference instead of that more straightforward word. Alternatively the abbreviation *q.v.*, short for *quod vide*, 'which see', may be found. In referring to its own pages a book may also use the words *supra* (above, i.e. previous) and *infra* (below).

(h) *cf*. This abbreviation stands for 'confer', meaning 'compare', and is a fairly well-known abbreviation. In some books it is replaced by *cp*.

These are the main abbreviations that need explaining. Other simpler abbreviations, such as e.g., will also be found, together with the abbreviations explained, in the section on 'Noting bibliographical information'. If there are any other abbreviations used, they should be explained elsewhere in the book. References to material in a foreign language, it may be noted, often include a translation of the title.

In certain circumstances references are abbreviated still further, just the chapter and page number of a book, for example, being given. The two most common types of such abbreviations are to the *Bible* and to lines of poetry. For example, when the reference I Chron. XII, 17, is met with, it is short for the *Bible*, first book of Chronicles, chapter 12, and verse 17. When a reference 2 Henry IV, v, ii, 46, is met with, in a book on Shakespeare, it is short for the play *Henry the Fourth*, the second part, the fifth act, the second scene, and line forty-six.

Before closing this section on 'Understanding bibliographical references', there are one or two remarks to be made on understanding the indexes of books. Most indexes are quite easily understood, though some of the abbreviations already explained may be met with. In books of more than one volume, the index will have to refer, of course, to a volume as well as to a page. This may be done by using roman numerals for the volumes, e.g. XI, 480, or the volume number may be indicated by the use of bold type, **11**, 480. Bold type is also used in indexes to indicate where the principal references to the subject occur as opposed to passing remarks on the subject. Some indication may be given in an index as to the place on a page where the information is to be found. This is most common in quick-reference books. For example, the *Encyclopaedia Britannica* divides each of its pages into quarters in the index, and refers to them by using the letters a, b, c, and d.

Bibliographies

The main use of bibliographies has already been discussed: it is to ascertain what material has been written on a subject. Bibliographies have additional uses; they enable the research worker to check on the details on books – for example, when they were published; and they enable him, especially if they comment on the books they list, to decide what books will be of most use to him.

Bibliographies can be grouped in several ways, depending upon the viewpoint of the observer; a grouping into three best serves the purpose of this chapter. The three groups are: bibliographies of bibliographies, general bibliographies and subject bibliographies. Bibliographies of bibliographies sounds a difficult phrase and yet it is self-explanatory. Instead of listing the books on a subject, they just list the bibliographies on that subject. They are the main kind of books about bibliographies, though guides to reference books and guides to research in particular subject fields also give considerable information about bibliographies. Some bibliographies of bibliographies, because of their importance to those beginning research, are described later in this chapter.

The second group, general bibliographies, consists of bibliographies covering all subjects in some way, and giving, for example, all the books published in a particular country. As general bibliographies are of value to all research workers, a few of them are described in the next section.

The third group, subject bibliographies, is by far the largest and it is outside the scope of this book to deal with it. It should be remembered that, so far as periodical articles are concerned, subject indexes to periodicals can be used as subject bibliographies. All large reference libraries will have a considerable number of subject bibliographies of which the following are representative examples: the *New Cambridge Bibliography of English Literature;* the *International Bibliography of Historical Sciences;* the *London Bibliography of the Social Sciences.*

BIBLIOGRAPHIES OF BIBLIOGRAPHIES

BESTERMAN, THEODORE. *A World Bibliography of Bibliographies.* 4th ed. Geneva, Societas Bibliographica, 1965–6. 5v. This is a most useful book, though it excludes bibliographies that appear in periodicals. Arranged by subject, with the fifth volume an index volume, it gives brief details about each bibliography, including the approximate number of books listed in it.

Bibliographic Index. (Three a year, cumulated.) New York, Wilson, 1938 to date. The issues of this periodical list bibliographies of all sorts. The arrangement is alphabetical by subject; there are no indexes.

COLLISON, R. L. W. *Bibliographies: Subject and National; a guide to their contents, arrangement and use.* 3rd ed. Crosby Lockwood, 1968. Compared with the previous two, this work is extremely selective. But, as it comments on most important bibliographies, it is worth consulting.

GENERAL BIBLIOGRAPHIES

British National Bibliography. (Weekly, cumulated.) Council of the BNB, 1950 to date. This is an important bibliography, as not only does it list virtually all books published in this country, but it arranges them by the Dewey classification scheme, and gives full catalogue details about them. The same Council publish the *British Catalogue of Music*, and from 1972 *Books in English*, a computer-based Anglo-American venture in micro-text form.

Cumulative Book Index. (Monthly, cumulated.) New York, Wilson, 1928 to date. The importance of this work is that it lists under author, title and subject books published in English throughout the world. Its coverage is best for books published in the United States.

HER MAJESTY'S STATIONARY OFFICE. *Catalogue of Government Publications*. (Daily.) HMSO, 1923 to date. This bibliography is rather more specialized than the others described, but it has been included as government publications are poorly covered in most general bibliographies. Cumulations are made of it both monthly and annually and, in addition, there are pub-lished lists devoted to individual government departments.

WHITAKER'S *Cumulative Book-list*. (Quarterly, cumulated.) Whitaker, 1924 to date. Gives, under author, title and broad subject, books printed and reprinted in this country. Unlike the *British National Bibliography*, which is aimed at librarians, it is intended for the use of the book trade. For even more up-to-date information, Whitaker's *Books of the Month and Books to Come* is available.

WHITAKER'S *British Books in Print*. (Annual.) Whitaker. Pre-viously known as the *Reference Catalogue of Current Literature*, this work lists under both author and title. The same publishers have also issued *Paperbacks in Print*, *Technical and Scientific Books in Print*, and *Children's Books in Print*.

BOOKS FOR FURTHER STUDY

BARZUN, J. and GRAFF, HENRY F. *The Modern Researcher*. Harcourt, Brace and World. Inc., 1957.
More comprehensive and of a better standard than its rivals.
BERRY, RALPH. *How to Write a Research Paper*. Pergamon, 1966.
WALFORD, A. J. and others. *Guide to Reference Material*. Revised ed. Library Association, 1966–1970. 3v.
Again of note as deals with bibliographies as well as the other types of quick-reference books.

Conclusion

These pages have tried to show the many ways in which libraries can be used. At the same time they have endeavoured to give the information readers need if they are to make the best use of libraries. I hope you have found this book of value. I also hope, however, that you will remember that this book should be followed up. There are four ways in which you can do this.

The first is by reading books which cover similar ground to this one, such as the four titles given at the end. The second is by reading, or at least examining, some of the books listed throughout under 'Books for further study'. These have been carefully chosen, but it must be admitted that there is little written on the subject of libraries which is suitable for library users as opposed to librarians. The third is by obtaining copies of the guides published by the libraries you use. It is to be regretted that some libraries have not yet issued guides of any description. The fourth and last way is by seeking the assistance of library staff. There are many points that can only be fully understood after a talk with a member of the staff.

Having indicated the four ways you can follow up the reading of these pages, it only remains for me to wish you every success in your use of libraries.

A SELECTION OF BOOKS ON USING LIBRARIES

The following four books have much to say on using libraries. The emphasis of each of them is different. Not one is like this book.

ATKINSON, FRANK. *The Public Library.* Routledge and Kegan Paul, 1970.
    Designed for children and limited to public libraries.
CAREY, R. J. P. *Finding and Using Technical Information.* Edward Arnold, 1966.

GATES, JEAN KEY. *Guide to the Use of Books and Libraries*. 2nd ed.
McGraw Hill, 1969.
Designed for American College students.
KYLE, BARBARA. *Teach Yourself Librarianship*. English University
Press, 1964.

Appendix
The Dewey Classification scheme: a subject guide

This Appendix shows the place at which the subjects most often required by readers appear within the scheme. It should be pointed out that libraries may not follow in every detail the scheme, and some do not use the latest edition of it (the eighteenth edition). There are, of course, many sub-divisions of most subjects listed. The names given to subjects are not always those given in the tables of the eighteenth edition as terms have been kept as simple as possible.

The arrangement of this Appendix is by ten subject-interest groupings. These are set out alphabetically, the headings chosen being named at the end of this paragraph. This type of arrangement has been chosen to complement (rather than duplicate) the arrangement of library catalogues. Within each of the ten headings, subjects are listed in alphabetical order. Some subjects will be found entered under more than one of the headings, others entered under more than one name.

Headings chosen for the subject-interest groupings:

Education and general
Hobbies and the home
Industry and business
Language and literature
Music and the arts
People and places
Religion and philosophy
Science and technology
Societies and nations
Sport and entertainment

EDUCATION AND GENERAL

Adult education	374
Bibliography	010
Careers	371.4, 331.7
Education	370

Encyclopaedias	030
Librarianship	020
Newspapers	070
Organizations and societies	060
Periodicals	050
Schools	371
Teaching	371
Universities	378

HOBBIES AND THE HOME

Antiques	745.1
Babies	618, 649
Card games	795.4
Cars	629.2, 796.7
Children	618, 649
Clothes	646, 677
Cookery	641.5
Decorating	643.7
Do-it-yourself	645, 690
Domestic animals	636
Dressmaking	646.4
Drink	641
Entertaining	641–642
Food	641
Furnishing	645, 684
Games	790
Gardening	635
Health	610, 649
Knitting	746.43
Medicine	610, 649
Motoring	629.2, 796.7
Pets	636
Photography	770
Reading	028
Sport	796–799

INDUSTRY AND BUSINESS

Accounting	657
Advertising	659.1
Agriculture	630
Air transport	387.7, 629.13
Banking	332.1

Business	650
Careers	371.4, 331.7
Commerce	380
Economics	330
Finance	332, 336
Industry	338, 660–690
Insurance	368
International trade	382
Investment	332.6
Labour	331
Management	658
Manufacturing	338, 660–690
Marketing	658.8
Metals	669
Money	332.4
Natural resources	333
Office services	651
Paper	676
Plastics	668.4
Postal services	383
Printing	686
Production	338
Railways	385, 625
Road transport	388, 629.2
Rubber	678
Shipping	386–387, 623.8
Shorthand	653
Textiles	677
Timber	674
Trade	380
Transport	385–388
Typing	652.3

LANGUAGE AND LITERATURE

Note: the second classification number, when there are two, refers to Literature.

American literature	810
Chinese	495.1, 895.1
Danish	439.81, 839.81
Dictionaries (English)	423
Drama (English)	822
Dutch	439.31, 839.31
English	420, 820

Essays (English)	824
Fiction (English)	823
French	440, 840
German	430, 830
Grammar (English)	425
Greek (Classical)	480, 880
Humour (English)	827
Italian	450, 850
Language	400
Latin	470, 870
Letters (English)	826
Literature	800
Norwegian	439.82, 839.82
Novels (English)	823
Plays (English)	822
Poetry (English)	821
Russian	491.7, 891.7
Spanish	460, 860
Speeches (English)	825
Swedish	439.7, 839.7

MUSIC AND THE ARTS

Antiques	745.1
Architecture	720
Art	700
Ballet	792.8
Ceramics	737
Cinema	791.43
Cinematography	778.5
Colour photography	778.6
Costume	391
Crafts	745–746
Drawing	740
Handicrafts	745–746
Interior decorating	747
Landscape art	710
Metalwork	739
Music	780
Numismatics	737
Opera	782
Painting	750
Photography	770
Planning	711

Scandinavia	914.8, 948
Scotland	914.1, 941
South America	918, 980
Spain	914.6, 946
Sweden	914.85, 948.5
Switzerland	914.94, 949.4
Travel	910
United Kingdom	914.2, 942
United States	917.3–917.9, 973–979
Wales	914.29, 942.9

RELIGION AND PHILOSOPHY

Bible	220
Christianity	220–280
Church (Christian)	260–280
Comparative religion	290
Customs and folklore	390
Ethics	170
Logic	160
Philosophy	100
Psychology	150
Religion	200
Supernatural	130
Theology (Christian)	230

SCIENCE AND TECHNOLOGY

Agriculture	630
Animals	590, 636
Anthropology	570
Astronomy	520
Atomic energy	539.7
Biology	574
Birds	598.2
Botany	580
Building	690, 720
Chemistry	540, 660
Civil engineering	624–628
Dentistry	617.6
Earth sciences	550
Electricity	537–538, 621.3
Engineering	620
Fishes	597, 799.1

Insects	595.7
Inventions	608
Life sciences	570
Mathematics	510
Mechanics	531–533, 621
Medicine	610
Meteorology	551.5
Metals	669
Natural history	570–590
Nuclear power	539.7
Paper	676
Physics	530
Plastics	668.4
Reptiles	598
Rubber	678
Science	500
Space science	629.4
Technology	600
Textiles	677
Wood	674
Zoology	590

SOCIETIES AND NATIONS

Air force	358.4
Anthropology	570
Army	356
Associations and societies	060
Biography	920
Civil service	351
Constitutional law	342
Crime	364–365
Criminal law	345
Customs and folklore	390
Economics	330
Etiquette	395
Geography	910
Government	320, 350
History	930–990
International law	341
International relations	327
International trade	382
Law	340
Local government	352

Nations	320, 350, 910, 930–990
Navy	359
Organizations	060
Parliament (British)	328.42
Political science	320
Public administration	350
Social sciences	300
Social services	360
Sociology	301
Statistics	310, 519
Statute law (British)	348
Welfare work	360

SPORT AND ENTERTAINMENT

Athletics	796.4
Ballet	792.8
Boxing	796.83
Card games	795.4
Cinema	791.43
Cricket	796.358
Dancing	793.3
Entertainment	790
Fishing	799.1
Football	796.33
Games	790
Golf	796.352
Horse riding and racing	798.2–798.6
Motor racing	796.7
Radio	791.44
Recreations	790
Sport	796–799
Swimming	797.2
Tennis	796.342
Television	791.45
Theatre	792

Index

Index